*Bob Proctor is one of the great and inspiring
speakers and communicators of all time.
Now his son Ray has put together 100 lessons to
absorb his Dad's brilliance in 90-second bite-sized
bits, so you have pure wisdom to
drink into your soul.*

–Mark Victor Hansen
Co-author of *Chicken Soup for the Soul*

*Bob Proctor's wisdom is invaluable and it is
fantastic to see his son Ray create a collection of the
life-changing lessons he's learned from his dad. The
Proctors are UNSTOPPABLE!*

–Cynthia Kersey
Bestselling Author of *Unstoppable & Unstoppable Women*

*What a wonderful book of wisdom to
help keep anyone focused on their goals
and self-improvement.*

–Arielle Ford
Author of *The Soulmate Secret:
Manifest the Love of Your Life with the Law of Attraction*
(Harper One, January 2009)

100

Lessons
from my Father

Dagmar,
My lunch friend!
:)

100

Lessons
from my Father

By Ray Proctor

LIFE SUCCESS PUBLISHING, LLC
8900 E Pinnacle Peak Road, Suite D240
Scottsdale, AZ 85255

Telephone: 800.473.7134
Fax: 480.661.1014
E-mail: admin@lifesuccesspublishing.com

ISBN: 978-1-59930-274-4

Cover :   Lloyd Arbour & LifeSuccess Publishing, LLC
Text: Lloyd Arbour & LifeSuccess Publishing, LLC

COMPANIES, ORGANIZATIONS, INSTITUTIONS, AND INDUSTRY PUBLICATIONS: Quantity discounts are available on bulk purchases of this book for reselling, educational purposes, subscription incentives, gifts, sponsorship, or fundraising. Special books or book excerpts can also be created to fit specific needs such as private labeling with your logo on the cover and a message from a VIP printed inside. For more information, please contact our Special Sales Department at LifeSuccess Publishing, LLC.

Printed in Canada

Dedication

To the memory of my father's mother, my Nan, Marguerite Proctor who we all admire with great affection for her persistent and positive "let's go" attitude. And to my beautiful wife, Toni, who shares with me an incredible life with our three wonderful boys, Curtis, Ben and Brian. The five of us cherish the countless memories of spending time with "Great Nan" in her Florida home. We miss her dearly, yet see her spirit every time we see my father.

Acknowledgements

Bob Proctor

I often joke that Thanksgiving Dinner at our house was a seminar because my dad really does live and breathe what he teaches. To him, it is not a job that he just leaves behind at the end of the day when he goes home. It is his life's purpose ... it is his life. The lessons in this book are a gift from him to all that read them. Dad teaches and studies continuously, day in and day out. Giving is his nature and I thank him most sincerely for unconditionally permitting me to use his material to create this book.

Gina Hayden

Gina has been at my father's side in business for more than 20 years. I am certain that I only know a fraction of what she has done for him over the years, but I do know she does an incredible job of keeping dad on schedule while organizing and archiving all of the material he creates. Thanks to Gina, the task of obtaining the transcripts from all of his radio shows was as easy as one exchange of emails.

Toni Proctor

Toni is my wife and the dearest friend I have ever known. I find her love and support to be immeasurably precious to me. Toni has never wavered in being all that a spouse can be and so much more. We share a warm, wonderful marriage where we enjoy just being together and, incredibly, in all our years as a couple, we have never argued nor experienced any form of animosity whatsoever. We do not compete with one another or demand anything from each other. We simply love, share and support one another.

Wendy Gallagher

Wendy's enthusiasm and excitement for this book has steered me in all the right directions with its concept. She is one of the most incredible people I have ever had the good fortune of working with. I am always entertained and fascinated with her wit, creativity and knowledge, but I am even more impressed with her integrity, dedication and work ethic. She knows how to earn trust.

Lloyd Arbour

Lloyd is excellent in his art of graphic design, but he is even better with his art of patience and tolerance. Thank you.

Wayne Collins

Wayne persistently reminded me of the tasks I needed to complete and ensured my words abided by the rules of proper English. Few people are truly skilled in the ability to write properly. It is people like Wayne who polish our words and usually go unnoticed. Wayne, your work is noticed. Thank you.

Introduction

I'm often asked what it's like to be the son of Bob Proctor. Obviously there are many answers to that question and not enough time or space in this book to reply!

But I do remember with great detail the day I thought of my dad as more than a very important man, who was recognized in airports and restaurants. It was the day I heard my father's voice on the radio. In my mind, he went from important to famous.

It was more than 20 years ago, when the radio show '90 Seconds with Bob Proctor' made its debut in Toronto. Hearing my father on radio not only impressed me, but my friends as well. Soon, I became known in my circle of friends as the guy whose dad was on the radio.

But more importantly, listening to my father's short but valuable words of wisdom had more impact than actually listening to him during one of his presentations or around the family dinner table. And as I would eventually learn, his inspiring words resonated with thousands of others.

You will learn volumes from attending Bob's seminars or studying his programs, but a few wise words delivered in just a short moment can be so targeted that they instantly expand your awareness. One of these spontaneous lessons can leave you contemplating a thought for days; it can have you seeing life from a whole new perspective. Once you gain greater awareness you can never lose it or give it back.

It is my father's ability to impart a great deal of wisdom with only a few short words that sets him apart from most educators. Those closest to him would say that some of the best education they have received from Bob was through his spontaneous advice.

While driving to work one day earlier this year, I began to think of one of my favourite pieces from my father's radio show, *The Unreasonable Person*. Then it struck me, that these radio scripts were sitting idle in boxes. It was then I knew I wanted to shake off the dust and bring these wonderful words to life, for all to enjoy.

My father's lessons are timeless as they are derived from authors he studied whose works were written decades, generations and even centuries ago. It is from reading, studying and applying that he acquired his knowledge. His lessons are a gift to you from his hard work. This book is available thanks to our LifeSuccess organization and the diligence of Gina Hayden who archived Bob's material for more than 20 years. My plan is for this book to be the first in a collection of four books from the *90 Seconds With Bob Proctor* material. I hope you enjoy it as much as thousands of others have who listened to my father on the radio. Take the time to study and grow.

Sincerely,

Ray Proctor

Accept the Challenge

Early in December I received a telephone call from Jay Jackson, VP of Redmond Broadcasting. He and his son had attended my seminar a few years ago, and he explained how the seminar had helped his son enjoy better marks in school. Furthermore, it had opened his son's mind to the idea he could earn an excellent income while he was still a student—which he did.

Jay suggested there were probably a number of people who would enjoy hearing some of the ideas from our seminars. The listening audience could benefit as he and his son had even if they were currently unable to attend seminars. I thought about it for a few minutes and then agreed to go on air the following month. After I agreed, he explained that I would need sixty-five shows recorded prior to the airdate. That almost caused me to change my mind as I was busy - very busy. We conduct our seminars all over the world, and I certainly was not looking for something to do. Nevertheless, I went ahead. When I considered changing my mind, I was thinking of the amount of work involved, not the opportunity or reward.

Today I would like to publicly thank Jay Jackson. It was Jay's idea for this show, *90 Seconds With Bob Proctor*. He has caused me to study more diligently, to exercise my mind while sitting on planes and in airports preparing new scripts. The show has since aired on a number of stations, and more people are benefiting from the idea, as is our seminar company.

When you are asked to do something, don't get caught in the trap of focusing on the work you must do. Think of the opportunity and rewards. I can assure you they could be numerous. Accept the challenge and do it!

Note from Author:

It is now my time to thank Jay Jackson. Although I do not believe I have ever met him, his challenge to my father years ago has had a lasting effect, which continues today with the book you now hold.

Mental Muscles

The leaders in business and industry all have at least one thing in common—they are mentally strong. Mental strength is an absolute prerequisite for a successful commercial career in our fast-moving world. Although there are relatively few people who develop mental strength, anyone can.

You are very aware of how to develop physical strength. You exercise the various muscles in your body by following a well-planned program, a program that is generally prescribed by a person who has developed an expertise in physical exercise.

You can follow the same basic principle to develop your mind. You simply follow an exercise program designed to strengthen your mental muscles.

People who have developed their mental muscles are very rarely, if ever, intimidated by challenging people or circumstances. They have what is commonly referred to as self-control. They are well-balanced, effective individuals.

At this point you may be wondering, "What are my mental muscles *and* how can I develop them."

Good questions. I can, and will, make you aware of what they are. However, I have yet to learn how to instruct a person to develop mental strength in ninety seconds. This is what our seminars have been doing for the past twenty-five years, and it usually takes a couple of days. I will do my best, however, to give you enough of an overview to get started.

You have six basic mental muscles, which are perfect; they only require exercise. Listen closely.

1. **Reason**

2. **Will**

3. **Intuition**

4. **Memory**

5. **Perception**

6. **Imagination**

Remember, I mentioned that they are perfect. There is no such thing as a bad memory, only a weak memory. You will astound yourself with what you can do with your marvelous mind with just a little exercise. Reason, will, intuition, memory, perception, imagination. Now, is your memory strong enough to remember them? There are only six to remember. I'm sure you can.

Reason

This is the first in a series of six shows dealing with your intellectual factors. The first I have chosen to speak about is reason. More specifically, your inductive reasoning factor— what a magnificent tool! This one gives you true freedom. Reason gives you the ability to choose your thoughts.

Victor Frankl, the great Viennese psychiatrist who spent years in concentration camps during the Second World War, wrote in his book *Man's Search for Meaning* that, regardless of the physical or intellectual abuse he received from his captors, they could not make him think something he did not choose to think.

Thinking is the highest function you are capable of, and this mental faculty should be exercised at every possible opportunity. Thought is the preamble to everything in your life.

All of the great leaders throughout history have told us we become what we think about. In fact, they have been in complete and unanimous agreement on this point while they disagree on almost every other point. Unfortunately, the vast majority of people rarely think; they simply accept what they see or hear.

The next time someone gives you a suggestion, rather than simply accepting and acting on the suggestion, *think*. Exercise your reasoning factor. Ask yourself if the suggestion will improve the quality of your life.

Here is another great exercise for your reasoning factor—one I am in the habit of using myself—that will give you most anything you want. Take a pad and pen. At the top of the pad write down something you want but in the past have not given serious thought to accomplishing. Begin to think of how you can get what you want without violating the rights of others. Disregard why you think you can't get what you want.

As simple as this exercise sounds, very few people do it. Most people think of what they don't want. As a result, they cheat themselves out of the good that life offers.

Think—think deep penetrating thoughts, and your reasoning factor will become strong.

The Will

This is the second in a series of six shows, and will deal with the intellectual factor, the human will. The will is the mental muscle that enables you and I to concentrate.

James Allen, a wonderful Victorian author, wrote about the will in his masterpiece, *As a Man Thinketh*.

> *The human will, that force unseen.*
>
> *The offspring of a deathless soul*
>
> *Can hew a way to any goal,*
>
> *Though walls of granite intervene.*

James Allen was correct. Your will is the mental faculty that gives genuine power to your ideas. The biographies and autobiographies of great men and women all indicate they had the ability to stay focused on their chosen objectives.

Napoleon said, "I see only the objective, the obstacle must give way." One of his biographers wrote that he had an immense capacity for sustained concentration. Another biographer once referred to him as "organized victory."

If you have a sincere desire to become mentally strong, you must exercise your will. It is absolutely essential that you develop your ability to concentrate. The most effective executives and all of the great salespeople have this outstanding ability. They are not easily distracted. Try and imagine a heart surgeon who has not developed the ability to give his or her undivided attention to the task at hand. I am certain you would not want to be that surgeon's patient.

Try this exercise every day for thirty days. Sit in your favorite chair and hold a candle in your hands. Light the candle and stare at the flame. If your attention begins wandering, immediately bring it back to the flame of the candle. If in the beginning you have difficulty keeping your mind focused, don't worry about it. Continue with this exercise four or five minutes at a time, two or three times a day. Within a month your ability to focus will become automatic.

This simple exercise can assist you in developing a very powerful will. Remember: concentration—intense concentration—gives real power to your ideas. When you begin to master your ability to concentrate on one thing, you can concentrate on virtually anything … and that's an invaluable skill to possess.

Intuition

Our topic for this segment is that mental faculty we all possess that is often referred to as our "sixth sense"—intuition. Intuition is that sensitive mental tool that gives us the ability to pick up another person's moods, thoughts, vibrations, and feelings. It's our "gut feeling," so to speak.

We often hear of a woman's intuition. For some reason, there is a popular belief that highly-developed intuitive abilities are peculiar to the female gender. There is absolutely no basis for this belief. Everyone has an intuitive factor, and anyone can certainly develop this mental faculty through exercise. The very effective salespeople, police detectives, customs agents, and so forth have a supersensitive intuitive factor. That is the very reason they are so effective. They've trained themselves to pick up the other person's energy as opposed to just hearing what the person is saying.

This has probably happened to you at least once in your lifetime. Think of the time someone looked into your eyes and told you they loved you … and you knew they were lying. Or, when you sensed something was wrong with a loved one, but they assured you everything was fine … only to find out later that they were, in fact, facing a serious problem. It was your intuitive factor that enabled you to pick up these unspoken messages.

To develop your intuitive factor and gain confidence in its use, you must have feedback. Whenever you are with people with whom you have built an excellent rapport, ask them for feedback. If you feel they are thinking about something, ask them. Your intuitive factor will actually pick up vibrations coming from those people. Quite often, if you have a very close relationship with someone, you will pick up what that person is thinking, even before they verbally express it to you.

Vibrations never lie. A person could be saying one thing yet thinking another. You will eventually reach the point where you pay closer attention to the vibrations you are receiving than the words you are hearing.

Intuition is one of the most valuable mental tools you possess. Begin to consciously use it. The rewards will be well worth the effort.

Note from Author:

When I would seek my father's advice on a dilemma he hardly ever gave me an answer or his opinion. He would ask me questions and in doing so would help me to think through my challenge. He would finish with "you already know the answer." He was right. I did know the answer but I just wasn't listening to my intuition. Now when people ask me for advice I often respond and say, "You already know the answer." They usually smile and agree.

Memory

Everyone has a perfect memory. There is no such thing as a poor memory—just an undeveloped memory.

The next time you catch yourself saying you forgot something, correct yourself immediately by telling yourself you didn't forget it—you just never remembered it in the first place.

Learning how to memorize names, places, or things is no more difficult than learning how to type or to drive a car. However, when you set out to learn how to drive a car, you knew it would take time, effort, and dedication. Before you got started, you had to make a decision to learn these skills and dedicate the time to acquiring them.

There are a number of wonderful books for sale that will assist you in the development of your memory. One I frequently recommend is *The Memory Book,* which shouldn't be too difficult to remember. *The Memory Book* is co-authored by Harry Lorayne and Gerry Lucas. By the way, the last I heard of Gerry Lucas, he was conducting a course on the West Coast teaching people to memorize the Bible.

On a number of occasions, I have worked with Harry Lorayne. The last time was at the Convention Centre in Toronto. To demonstrate what could be done with our memory, he had memorized the present week's copy of *Time* magazine—the entire magazine, verbatim. He held the audience spellbound. Then he proceeded to explain that he has no special powers; anyone could learn to do what he had done. Buy his book and practice.

Memory is developed not just through association, but ridiculous association. For example, if you parked your car in garage area L2, to remember its location, use your imagination to build a ridiculous picture in your mind of yourself leaving the car in space L2. See yourself kissing the car goodbye saying, "I love you." The car kisses you back saying, "I love you too." Sounds ridiculous, doesn't it? It is, and it works. Buy Harry's book *The Memory Book*.

Note from Author:

I can't even begin to count how many exams I completed in university or Professional Designation courses where using the ridiculous association or peg memory system helped me sail through the tests. I still use it today when I am without pen and paper to remember tasks I need to complete.

Perception

I am certain you will agree that your attitude has a strong influence on your success in all areas of your life. Your perception of a situation will determine your attitude.

Ideas, buildings, places, and things can be viewed from many different points of view. Each time you alter your point of view, your perception will change, possibly dramatically. This is neither good nor bad and yet it could be either. Your perception will be the determining factor.

Most of our disagreements have their cause in perception. Two individuals who are discussing a particular situation and are in complete disagreement should thoroughly check their perceptions of the situation. It is quite possible they are, in fact, not discussing the same situation at all. Different perceptions, different situation.

You could be holding yourself back from an exciting position or a dynamic career because of your perception of what you can do. Many potentially great salespeople remain stuck selling small-ticket items because of their perception of what it would take to sell the big ones. What they need to do is investigate further. The more information you gather about a place, a thing, a person, or a situation, the more you will find your perception of it changing.

The next time you find yourself thinking of something you would like to do, but holding back because you think you can't, activate this mental faculty. Another point of view may present the right road to a bright future for you. Similarly, if you are disagreeing with a person, attempt to see the situation from their point of view.

Someone once lamented to Dr. Maxwell Maltz that he was bankrupt, ruined, and disgraced. Dr. Maltz said, "The fact is, you are bankrupt. It is your perception of the situation that causes you to feel ruined and disgraced."

Perception is a great mental tool; use yours to improve your view of life.

Imagination

This is the last of six segments dealing with your intellectual factors. Oddly enough, it is also the sixth law in Napoleon Hill's *Law of Success*. Hill writes, "You will never have a definite purpose in life; you will never have self-confidence; you will never have initiative and leadership unless you first create these qualities in your imagination and see yourself in possession of them."

Just as the oak tree develops from the germ that lies in the acorn, and the bird develops from the germ that lies asleep in the egg, so will your achievements grow out of the organized plans that you create in your imagination. Imagination is the mental faculty out of which your visions arise.

All the great achievers of the past have been visionary figures. They built grand images in their minds and then acted with courage until their images materialized in their lives.

The uninitiated look at this form of mental activity as daydreaming or fantasizing. They don't seem to realize that all of the wonderful conveniences they are presently enjoying were, at one time, nothing but an image in someone else's mind.

Napoleon Hill wrote in his best-selling book, *Think and Grow Rich*, that your imagination is the most marvelous, miraculous, inconceivably powerful force the world has ever known.

Practice using your imagination to form beautiful pictures in your mind of what you would like your life to be like. Understand that an image in your mind is the first stage of the creative process in life. You are a creative being.

Look at whatever you are doing today and imagine how you could do it better, how you could do it faster, how you could be much more effective. Formulate the plans for the successful execution of your new image. Understand this beautiful truth: you will never form a picture of something you seriously want if you lack the ability to execute the image. You are a powerful, creative being. Enjoy it.

Note from Author:

Every time the words *Think and Grow Rich* roll off my father's tongue, I think of Uncle Ray. Raymond Douglas Stanford was not my uncle, but a special friend of my father's. He is the gentleman who gave my dad *Think and Grow Rich*. In doing so he changed my father's life and, in turn, countless others. Having someone name their child after you has to be an incredible honour. I was given Raymond Douglas's name and that is something that makes me very proud. We lost Uncle Ray on my seventh birthday, but he is clearly still with us today.

"You are the only problem you will ever have, and baby you are the only solution."

–Raymond Douglas Stanford

Mental Strength

A few weeks ago I did a show on mental strength. I pointed out how we are all very familiar with physical strength and how, through a proper exercise program, you and I can develop our physical muscles. I also indicated that mental strength could be developed by exercising our mental muscles.

The world respects and rewards the individual who has become mentally strong. If you were to study the lives of those people who, in the past or present, have achieved what may be considered greatness in any given field, you would arrive at the inevitable conclusion that every one of them was a mental giant. These people are confident of their own abilities. Very rarely, if ever, do these people find it necessary to become defensive.

If you saw the movie *Patton*, you will remember George C. Scott's Academy Award winning performance as General Patton. The movie began with the famous general addressing his troops prior to leading them into battle.

It was a short, but powerful speech he gave. In it, the general stated that he did not want any messages coming back that they were holding their positions. He said, "We're not holding anything; we are advancing constantly." Those words were the expression of a powerful mind.

That is the kind of strength we want to advance constantly in our business and in our lives—and we can! Practice the mental exercises mentioned in the six previous sections. It might take a few minutes every day, but you will be rewarded for the rest of your life.

600 Hours to Study

Have you ever figured out how much of your life you spend sitting behind the wheel of your vehicle? If you drive your car 25,000 miles in a year, you are behind the steering wheel somewhere between 500 and 600 hours. What do you do with all this time? You are either wasting it or investing it wisely.

If, in the coming year, you knew you would have between twelve and fifteen, forty-hour weeks that you could devote to improving your ability in any area of your life you considered important, what would you study? Think about this. You can turn your automobile into a learning center.

The other day I had reason to drive to Rochester, New York and back. I could have flown, but I decided to drive. For seven hours I listened to exciting recordings from a convention held by the National Speakers Association. I heard a number of great speeches; the time went by quickly, and I acquired a few ideas that I know will improve my business.

You could learn a language in a relatively short period of time, even if you only studied the language while you were driving. Time has become very important. Successful people are forever attempting to make better use of their time. It is much like the dollar bill—once you have spent it, you cannot get it back.

Personally, I have been using my driving time to develop my potential ever since tape decks were first installed in automobiles. It has become a habit. I could add that it is one of the most valuable habits I have. It would be difficult to think of a subject you could not study while driving. Six hundred hours is a long time. Choose to use it wisely.

Choices

Last week I had a two-hour layover in the Los Angeles airport. I still had fourteen or fifteen hours of flying time ahead of me, so I decided to pick up a good book. Fortunately, I selected a classic. It was a book by Pocket Books written by Shad Helmstetter, titled *Choices: Discover Your 100 Most Important Choices*.

Helmstetter writes about choosing not to complain:

"Imagine the incredibly powerful, productive moments, minutes and hours of the days and weeks of our lives that we could complain or not—simply by our own choices. I doubt that we could accurately calculate the amount of additional productive time each of us would have in one year if, for that year, we turned every moment of complaint into a moment of choice to do something better instead.

"Imagine what we could do in our homes, with our families and in our personal lives if we made the choice to replace complaining with positive belief. Imagine what you could do with those extra moments and hours of your life if you made the choice, right now, to never complain—and at every opportunity from here on out to replace even the most minor complaint with the positive energy of your own potential.

"Imagine never again complaining. Could you still be a strong person, a person of conviction and opinion? Would you still do everything you need to do to make change in your life, or to deal in a clear and effective way with the obstacles and problems that come along? The answer is that you would be more effective, as you would be concentrating on positive actions to improve situations."

Those are not the words of some motivational speaker or an inspirational message. They are simply the truth.

How to Love What You Do

This past week I was out of town on a business trip with one of my associates. Somehow, the subject of different people and their various professions became the topic of our conversation. As we talked about each of the different types of work, I would comment, "I wouldn't want to do that." Finally, my associate said, "Let's face it, Bob. You wouldn't be happy doing anything other than what you are doing." I thought about that for a moment, smiled, and agreed.

Then I sat there and permitted my mind to drift back a number of years to when I first began working. I almost always wished I was doing what someone else was doing. It seemed I was never happy with the job I had.

What happened? What changed? That is a good question, and a great lesson is contained in the answer.

Earl Nightingale answered that question in a speech he made many years ago. The title of his speech was, "The Business Got Into Me." Earl told a story about a successful businessman and what it was that moved him into the success column.

The businessman explained how he got into the business with his company twenty years ago. For the first couple of years nothing much happened. He was very average—not too happy—until one day the business got into him. From that time on, he explained, it was great.

The man suggested that it isn't when we get into the business that is important—it is when the business gets into us. As I thought about my own situation, I could relate to Earl Nightingale's message and his friend's advice.

I had spent a number of years waiting for the business to prove itself to me. I had the equation reversed. I had to prove myself to the business. The business would give me what I asked for.

Yes, I feel I am in the greatest profession in the world, and I love what I do. What happened? You guessed it! The business got into me.

How do you like what you do?

The Unreasonable Person

The reasonable person adapts himself to the world;
the unreasonable one persists in trying to adapt the
world to himself. Therefore, all progress depends on
the unreasonable person.

—George Bernard Shaw

If I were to paraphrase what Shaw wrote, I suppose I could say people are considered reasonable when they are content with the way things are presently. However, when we encounter a person who is dissatisfied with the status quo and endeavors to change it, he or she is frequently considered to be unreasonable.

This concept takes me back to a time when I was a young boy. My grandmother played an important role in my upbringing. She was continually telling me I should be satisfied with what I had.

My grandmother was a real Angel of God in my mind, but as I look back on those days, I realize there were a number of points she attempted to sell me where she was wrong. This was one of those points. There is absolutely nothing wrong with being dissatisfied; in fact, there is a lot of good to be derived from a mind that is dissatisfied.

It was dissatisfaction that caused Edison to light up the world, Ford to give us the automobile, the Wright brothers to introduce us to a new kingdom, and Bell to enable us to speak to someone on the other side of the globe. All of these great advances were brought to us because their inventors were, as many believed, unreasonable. The beautiful truth is these inventors were dissatisfied.

37

If you are disagreeing with a present situation just to disagree, you are very likely unreasonable. However, if you are diligently attempting to improve a situation, absolutely refuse to permit someone else's remark that you are unreasonable to dissuade you. Be unreasonable in their minds, but move ahead; in the long haul they will very likely follow you.

Develop the Ben in You

Everyone has some Ben in them. When you develop it, the world will see it and reward you for it.

The name "Ben" triggers an image in my mind of human decency, kindness, enthusiasm, and genuine generosity. These qualities we all possess; however, with most of us they need a little developing.

Ben Culotta worked with me for five years. Everyone knew him as Ben or Benny. I use the word "knew" because Ben was taken from us suddenly.

He had the best attitude of anyone I have ever known. Numerous times when I have been speaking to audiences all over the world about the importance of a good attitude, I have used Ben as an example of what we should all strive for. I have also said every company should have a Ben.

Develop the Ben in you. Your company, your friends, your family, and you will live in a better world. A company full of Bens would be something to see!

All the years I knew Ben, I never heard him complain about anything, and I know for a fact many times he had cause to complain loudly.

Every morning when he came into the office where we worked, he would walk around with a big smile on his face and shake everyone's hand. Almost everyone received a compliment as well. Ben knew how to make you feel good.

Ben never criticized anyone, and if he was present when someone else was being critical, he would quietly excuse himself.

Nothing was too much trouble for Ben. He was the most willing and unselfish person I have been privileged to know in over half a century. It is personalities like Ben Culotta we should all emulate. Let's begin today.

Note from Author:

We still speak of Ben Culotta today. When we do, the mention of his name always brings a serene smile to everyone's face.

Poise

Poise is a large contributor to success, and, indeed, there can be little success without poise. Poise is keeping your head when everybody else loses theirs. Poise is power, square-jawed and firmly set. When blame seems to come your way, when the fingers of fault-finders all seem centered in front of your face, when failure after failure files through your door, when former friends turn into foes, when clouds creep onward, black and threatening—then is the time for poise. Then is the time to face the crowd and fill the air with your command of confidence and poise. The cool heads are the battle winners.

And you who are ruling and conserving through the art of poise, you are preserving peace by being prepared for war. The strong person always listens and thinks. In such an attitude he or she can consider and weigh with justice and rare freedom the most puzzling problems. Poise to such a person is like a bank full of funds.

Poise infused in your character will balance it—make it fit and formidable.

How many times have you seen the person of action at his or her desk, calm and collected, with plenty of time for anything important, while all about that person is confusion and a frantic air that is, after all, charged with very little importance.

Study poise and train yourself in it. Poise starts when you begin to eliminate fear and disorder.

George Matthew Adams wrote an article on poise in 1913. I have read it over many times and found it quite helpful. Poise is a human quality that time cannot alter. Poise always has and always will, benefit those who develop it.

Earnest Desire

Wallace D. Wattles said, "Desire is the effort of the unexpressed possibility within, seeking expression without, through your actions."

Permit me to dissect that powerful statement. "Desire is the effort of unexpressed possibility within." We all have aspirations, dreams, and goals. Desire is the energy exercised within; it's the energy applied to your dream or goal that seeks to manifest itself on the physical level through what you do—your behavior.

Affirmations are the mental tools you use to alter your old conditioning and firmly fix your chosen *wants* in your subconscious mind. Only then does it become an earnest desire.

Thought is the fuel that creates the steam that turns your wheel of fortune. Do you want beauty in your life? Could you use a dose of inspiration? Would you like prosperity in your life? If so, create an earnest desire through affirmations. By using affirmations of wonderful, prosperous, successful thoughts consistently enough, they will become part of you. What you are doing is changing yourself by making yourself what you want to be.

It's just not possible to dwell on negative, limiting, small, and poverty-stricken mental pictures for eight or ten hours a day and expect to win. You need to stop feeding the evils you don't desire and focus, through affirmations, on the good you do desire. Repeat to yourself over and over again statements like,

"I am a prosperous person."

"I matter."

"I am lovable and capable."

"I am confident and happy."

If you tell yourself a lie often enough, you will begin to believe it. When I began to make changes in my own life—some thirty-five, forty years ago, that's what I had to do. I had to lie to myself. The person I wanted to become was so far removed from the person I was, it was the only thing I could do if I wanted to make any permanent change. I focused on the very opposite behavior of what I was in the habit of doing and began to affirm. That's what you're doing when you start repeating affirmations—you're actually telling yourself a lie to make it become the truth.

Wattles also said, "Do small things in a great way, every day." Writing an exciting, big idea in the form of a goal is something great. Do it every day, and you will create an earnest desire. That earnest desire must, and will, manifest itself in your life.

Room of Mirrors

The other day I was speaking with a dear friend who was sharing her situation with me, and it wasn't exactly pleasant. Her husband was very unhappy, critical of everyone and everything. He didn't want to go anywhere or do anything. She explained that he acted as if everyone and everything were against him.

The lady's description of her husband reminded me of something that I read years ago about the person whose mind was like a room with mirrored walls. It wouldn't matter which way he looked: all he would ever see was himself and his situation. He would not be able to invoke the law of relativity. Not being able to compare his life with most of the world's population, he would never know that, by comparison, he was living much like Solomon in all his splendor and glory.

Actually, this man's down-and-out attitude was caused by thinking only of himself. Most, if not all, of his problems would be solved if he replaced the mirrored walls of his mind with windows. Then he would see what an absolutely fascinating world we live in—full of color, interesting people, and opportunity. There would be so many challenging things to do and places to go that he would forever be scrambling for time.

When individuals supersensitive jump to conclusions, and allow themselves to be negative, they are showing their immaturity. By replacing the mirrors with windows, this high level of sensitivity can be converted into awareness, and negative impressions can be made to serve as a stimulus for creative thought. This, in turn, will lead to happiness, peace of mind, and a fulfilled life.

Ideas

"Never tell a young person that something cannot be done. God may have been waiting for centuries for somebody ignorant enough of the impossible to do that very thing." That advice was given to us by John Andrew Holmes, and it's excellent advice.

Virtually every success story has hidden in it a part where the creator of the idea was told to take that crazy idea and get lost—that it could never be done. Victor Hugo once said, "There is nothing as powerful as an idea whose time has come." Ideas do not only transform your business, they can transform your life. The good thing about ideas is they're free and you have the ability to create them!

Albert Einstein pointed out that imagination is more important than knowledge. Why? Well, when you examine it, you'll come to find that it's because knowledge is limited whereas imagination is not.

The most important capital asset in your business is not equipment, buildings, money, investments or any of the other things we may think. The more important asset we have is our ideas. Anyone can come up with ideas. If you doubt this, consider all of the ways some of your most non-productive people think of to get out of work. And if that doesn't convince you, get a few of your people together and brainstorm solutions to a current problem that you feel is blocking progress in your company. You will be amazed at how creative some of the people surrounding you actually are.

Innovative people have always been in high demand. Help those around you to develop that never-say-die attitude by developing it yourself. Make a decision today to outlaw complaining, whining, and negative thinking in your own personality. And, a word of caution: if and when you are criticized for being so positive or as some call it, unrealistic, you will know you are on the right track.

One of the most favored arguments of these naysayers is that there is no market for this in today's economy. Be aware that the economy is not meant to control us ... we are meant to control the economy.

Conflict

One of the most difficult tasks you or I will face in life is overcoming the internal conflicts that rage within us. Do it, don't do it; do it, don't do it. You recognize what I am referring to.

Every conflict is a set of opposing ideas. All of us have experienced knowing what we should do on the one hand, and doing what we feel like doing on the other. By understanding these two opposing forces warring within us, we come to an awareness of the truth; we no longer remain slaves. A clear understanding will make us masters over ourselves.

In the Bhagavad Gita it is written, "A man's own self is his friend. A man's own self is his foe."

Oscar Wilde spoke out on this when he asked, "Why was I not told that my brain could hold, in one tiny ivory cell, both God's heaven and God's hell?" A good question, isn't it?

David Seabury explained that modern science knows much about such conflicts. We call the mental state that engenders it ambivalence, a collision between thought and feeling.

The more you learn about the workings of your marvelous mind, the better position you will be in to take control over your life. The Victorian author James Allen offered us excellent advice when he suggested, "He who would be useful, strong, and happy must cease to be a passive receptacle for the negative, beggarly, and impure streams of thought. As a wise householder commands his servants and invites his guests, so must he learn to command his desires and to say, with authority, what thoughts he shall admit into the mansion of his soul."

Set Yourself Free

Do you think of Shakespeare as being a highbrow author who wrote plays designed to bore high school students? Do you view his writings as something for other people—writings that had nothing to do with the practical problems of life? If your answer is yes, think again. Shakespeare was not a way out, but a way in kind of guy.

I quote, "Every bondman in his own hand bears the power to cancel his captivity." How can you apply his advice in a practical manner to today?

"Every bondman." What does he mean? All individuals who feel they are in bondage in any way—who feel trapped by circumstances; who seem bound to failure, poverty, and sickness; who seem held back from what would make their life complete and good.

"Every bondman bears in his own hand." Those who feel trapped possess within themselves the power to cancel, or get rid of, their captivity, their seeming bondage.

You can be free. You have the power within you to remove the shackles that bind you.

Paul Carus wrote in *The Gospel of Buddha*, "People are in bondage because they have not removed the idea of 'I.'"

Leland Val Van De Wall wrote, "Let us not look back in anger, nor forward in fear, but around us in awareness."

The only power our problems can have over us is the power we give to them. As Emerson wrote, "The only thing that can grow is the thing we give energy to."

If you are in bondage, held captive by problems, you have the power in your own hands to set yourself free. You are the *only* one who can set yourself free.

Shakespeare said it, I believe it, and that settles it … for me.

Failing Is Winning

Do you ever get tired of failing? I'm sure you do. I most certainly do. However, if you think about it, there is only one clear alternative, and that alternative is certainly not acceptable to me: it's quitting, giving up, and not trying any more.

Many misguided individuals try something once or twice, and, if they do not hit the bulls-eye, they feel they are failures. Failing does not make anyone a failure, but quitting most certainly does.

Every day you hear about a ball player signing a contract that will pay him a few million dollars a year. You should try to keep in mind that this same player misses the ball more often than he hits it when he steps up to the plate.

Everyone remembers Babe Ruth for the 714 home runs he hit, and they rarely mention that the man struck out 1,330 times. Do you think he wandered around with his head hanging because he failed 1,330 times or because he struck out more often than any other player?

Charles F. Kettering once said in a speech he was making, "When you're inventing, if you flunk 999 times and succeed once, you're in."

That is true of just about any activity you can name. There are exceptions, but the world will soon forget your failures in light of your achievements. Don't worry about failing; it will toughen you up and get you ready for your big win.

Success is simply moving toward your goal. Work at improving and form the attitude that all really successful people possess. They fail, but they never submit to failure because they are successful! The key word here is *submit*. Never submit to failure, and you will always be a winner!

Following the Crowd

The most natural thing in the world for you to do in life is probably the most destructive insofar as succeeding at anything is concerned. That is following the crowd. Historically, the crowd has always been traveling in the wrong direction.

Ninety-eight out of a hundred people who start a new job look around to see how everyone else is doing their job, and they follow suit. If you are starting a new job, you should look around and ask yourself if any of these people know what they are doing. Then, consider going to the boss and asking who the most effective employees in the company are. If you're going to follow people, follow them.

Eighty percent of the production that counts is being done by 20 percent of the people. It necessarily follows that 80 percent of the money paid to employees is paid to that 20 percentile group.

It is not uncommon in a sales force of twenty or thirty people to have one or two salespeople selling more than all the rest combined. If you're in sales, find out what those two are doing that is so different. It may be making one extra call per day.

There are millions of golfers and thousands of pros but only a few who play the game like Arnold Palmer and Gary Player. These top performers are not lucky; they're dedicated.

You were encouraged to be like the other kids when you were young. You have been conditioned to follow the crowd. In many schools, you are even dressed like the other kids.

Well, you're not a child any longer, and you're not like the other kids. You are unique. That is what makes the Mona Lisa so valuable: there is only one. There is also only one of you. Be yourself; break away from the crowd.

Success

There is a word in your vocabulary that has to be the most abused and misunderstood word in the English language. This word is used to describe what most people want and spend their lives looking for. It is available to everyone with very little effort, and costs nothing; your age and station in life are definitely not factors, yet only about 3 percent of us have ever found it.

You guessed it, the word is *success*. What is success? That is a good question. I have read thousands of definitions, but I have yet to find a better one than the definition I received from Earl Nightingale close to thirty years ago.

"Success is the progressive realization of a worthy ideal." If you know where you are and where you are going, and you are progressively moving your life in the direction of your dream or goal, then you are successful. Only 3 percent of the people you are surrounded by have a clearly-defined goal written in a definite statement. Most individuals wander through life dreaming, and they go to their graves with their dreams still inside them. Decide what you want. Write it out and get moving. Be successful.

Challenge Yourself

When I was a youngster in school, I participated in track and field. Pole-vaulting was my specialty; it was the one event I seemed to do much better than others.

I clearly remember sending that crossbar flying more often than I cleared it. I also remember being very critical of myself when that happened. I suppose knocking the bar off left me with a feeling that I had failed, that I had missed the mark. Unfortunately, nobody ever advised me any differently.

Looking back today, years older and hopefully much wiser, I often wish that someone had helped me and my friends to understand that we weren't failing when we knocked the crossbar off—we were succeeding. Every time we did make it over the bar, the teacher would raise it to a new height, and for the next few vaults the bar would go flying again, which was actually a good thing. In reality, it caused us to stretch, to do more than we thought we could do. Had the coach left it at the same height, in a short time we would have been clearing the bar without effort and would have probably lost interest in the sport. There wouldn't have been any challenge left in it for us.

As I mentioned earlier, Earl Nightingale once explained, "Success is the progressive realization of a worthy ideal." Although reaching the goal is always a rewarding experience, it's not success in itself. Success is moving toward the goal; it is the obstacles we face and the lessons we learn by going beyond what we think we can do. When we were knocking down the crossbar, we were attempting to reach the goal and were stretching, giving it everything we had. That could hardly be considered failing.

Ray Proctor

Every time we ran down the field, lowering the pole into the box and trying to vault ourselves over the bar, we were challenging ourselves. That, in itself, is the only useful purpose of a goal. When you challenge yourself, you are bringing more of yourself to the surface. If you knock the bar flying today, go at it again—you're definitely moving in the right direction. You're a success!

Environment

I'd like to share a few ideas with you about your environment. I am not referring to the air or the forests; I am thinking about the people who surround you.

Karl Menninger of the Menninger Foundation once said that your environment was more important than your heredity. In my opinion he is correct.

The people you associate with and surround yourself with have a lot to do with the type of person you become. Statistically, it's been proven that many people receiving welfare assistance are third and fourth generation welfare recipients. I've also been told that the incidence of convicted repeat offenders who are returned to prison runs around 80 to 90 percent. That said, there are many who break out of their environment and work toward a better life.

In a speech he gave, Howard Bonnel was illustrating a point in reference to your income being connected to your environment. Bonnel said that if you do not earn 100K per year it is probably because you never mix with anyone who does, so you never hear anyone talking about it. I believe there is a fair amount of truth in that statement.

Any achiever will agree it is a sound idea to choose your associates carefully. Pick people who set a great example and who are involved in big ideas. Actively listen to what they have to say and observe their behavior closely. The salesperson who studies the actions of the superstar salespeople in their particular industry or the student who observes and learns from the honor student—these individuals improve their results.

Understand that if someone else's results are superior to yours, they have simply learned to utilize more of their potential than you have.

Carefully review your environment. You might find that you are associating with people who have a tendency to pull you down. You know the old adage: birds of a feather flock together. That doesn't mean they're bad people, but if you really want to break out of that pattern of negativity and make something happen in your life, I'd suggest you carefully consider your surroundings. Search out people who are making it happen and learn from them.

Close Those Doors

In 1949, a young fifteen-year-old sophomore student from Plainfield High School in New Jersey made a decision to become the greatest athlete in the world. It was a pretty ambitious objective—an idea that most fifteen year olds wouldn't even dream about. But Milt Campbell has proved to the world he was no ordinary fifteen-year-old.

You see, Milt had been studying the life of the man whose picture was on the back of the Wheaties box, Bob Mathias. Bob had won the gold medal in the decathlon competition at the Olympic Games in London, England, in 1948.

Mathias' success inspired Campbell, who began to train his mind and body to do what Bob Mathias had done. Milt started to visualize himself standing on the top step, having the gold hung around his neck in Helsinki at the Olympic Games in 1952. He worked hard and trained hard. Milt gave the best he had, and, just as he predicted, off he went to Helsinki. He had earned the right to be one of the athletes to represent his country in the decathlon.

Unfortunately, Mathias wasn't satisfied with the gold he had from the London Games. Bob Mathias wanted another gold medal, and he got it. Campbell had to settle for silver, but he didn't quit. Standing on the second step, Milt Campbell laid claim to the gold that would be handed out four years later in 1956 at the Olympic Games in Melbourne, Australia. Because he wouldn't quit, Milt Campbell earned the gold; he realized the dream he carried in his mind for eight years.

Prior to writing this script, I had just finished a telephone conversation with Milt. He and I were arranging to meet in Atlantic City next week where we are speaking at a conference. As I always do when I'm talking with Milt, I asked what lesson he learned from his experience. He said he had many opportunities to quit. It was tough. With every worthwhile goal, it's the same: a door will always open to let you out gracefully. You must close that door and keep focused. Don't ever quit. Milt Campbell didn't, and he earned the gold.

Note from Author:

Milt has been a friend of my father's for many years. He is still an incredibly fit man. We often refer to Milt when laughing about how active my dad is at the age of 74. We joke and say even Milt can't keep up to him in the airports!

Don't Think in Reverse

You will never obtain any measure of material wealth if you insist upon living your life as if you were looking back through the rearview mirror of an automobile. Nevertheless, this seems to be a common error that many people have turned into a habit. Remember the old adage, which says, let the dead bury the dead. Stop looking back in your life and worrying about things that have already occurred and can no longer be altered. Pursuing that kind of mental activity will never lead to anything worthwhile in your life.

You should understand, moreover, that all of the great achievers of the past have been visionary figures. They were men and women who projected into the future and did not belabor the past. They thought of what could be rather than what already was, and then they moved themselves into action, bringing these things to fruition.

Leland Val Van De Wall offers some excellent advice on this subject. "Let us not look back in anger, nor forward in fear, but around us in awareness."

If you have been guilty of allowing your sales sheets, your bank account, or the X-rays the doctor takes of your body to control the way you view your sales, financial position, or health, you will never see any marked improvement in your life in any of these areas. However, if you let the present, physical results serve only as an indication of the images that you have been holding in the past and then proceed to look into the bright future and to build an image of the good that you desire, you will see the image materialize.

Look up, look ahead, and form the image of the life you choose to live.

Note from Author:

Leland Val Van De Wall was one of my father's key mentors. He exuded calmness and wisdom. He was a walking example of the last chapter, Serenity, in *As a Man Thinketh*. We lost Val a few years ago but we continue to experience his wisdom in my dad's teachings.

The Obstacle Course

Obstacles are something everyone encounters in life. The trick of a successful life is to conquer the obstacles as they appear.

I can vividly remember doing my basic training in the navy many years ago. We would get hauled out of bed at a ridiculous hour and marched in the cold to an obstacle course. I was very young at the time and never understood what the navy was doing or why they were doing it. At the time it appeared to me as if my government had hired people who had a sadistic streak and paid them to design these obstacle courses. I honestly believed they were trying to kill us.

Looking back today, hopefully much wiser and certainly much richer from those experiences, I realize they were trying to toughen us up—make men out of boys. The obstacles were causing my peers and me to get in touch with something within us we didn't even know was there.

There is something else of real value I can see today that I totally missed years ago. Although there was always a certain amount of hostility felt by everyone prior to these marches, it was an enthusiastic group that returned—tired but enthused. We had accomplished something; we conquered the obstacles. The leaders we referred to as sadistic prior to the march suddenly turned into good guys when we returned victorious. They were the same people with whom we were laughing and joking.

If you are in the middle of what appears to be an obstacle course today, reach out to meet the obstacles. Conquer them and I guarantee you will see yourself as a stronger, wiser, and happier person.

Fear of Success

Subconscious conditioning prevents many people from achieving and enjoying the success that could be theirs. How many people have you met, worked with, or are related to who you were certain would make tomorrow's headlines—individuals who showed great potential but who never realized their great expectations. These fallen stars very likely have suffered from fear of success.

You may think this is ridiculous; how could a person possibly have a fear of success? It is caused by conditioning—subconscious conditioning, and it is one of the most disastrous of all fears we experience in our lifetime. This fear prevents people from achieving their maximum potential. It limits their foresight and causes them to set goals that have no emotional value. It prevents people from attaining their production possibilities.

A common symptom of this conditioning is when people believe they should not be doing as well as they are doing. They think they are experiencing too much success too quickly. When a windfall comes their way, they feel it is too good to last.

If you recognize what I am describing in yourself, if you experience short bursts of success only to fall back into an old, not quite so successful pattern, the odds are pretty good that your subconscious conditioning needs a little working on.

Permit me to suggest that you get Dr. Joseph Murphy's excellent book *The Power of Your Subconscious Mind*. Studying it could prove to be a liberating experience. This is a book that has a special place in my library and probably should in yours as well.

A Message to Garcia

Garcia was a Cuban lawyer who became a revolutionary general. He commanded a Cuban army against Spain in the revolt of 1885 to 1888 preceding the Spanish-American War.

President McKinley wanted to know what aid the United States should send to Cuba but had no way of contacting General Garcia as he was at an undisclosed location in the mountains of Cuba. At the suggestion of one his aides, President McKinley summoned a young United States lieutenant, Andrew S. Rowan. He handed him a sealed envelope and instructed him, "Carry this message to Garcia."

At the time, Rowan did not ask, "Who is Garcia? Where is Garcia? How will I find him? How do I get there? Are you sure he's still alive?" Rowan simply took the message, sealed it in an oilskin pouch, strapped it over his heart, and, in four days, landed by night off the coast of Cuba from an open boat. He disappeared into the jungle and three weeks later arrived on the other side of the island, having traversed a hostile country on foot and delivered his letter to Garcia.

In my opinion, Rowan's form should be cast in bronze and placed on every college campus. In all of our learning, mighty few have learned how to "carry a message to Garcia." The concentrated effort that it would have taken this young man to accomplish his all-important task would have been incredible!

If you are in management, put this matter to a test. Ask someone in your office to look in the encyclopedia and write a brief article on the life of Garcia.

I'll bet that the person will look at you as if you've lost your mind. What for? What encyclopedia? Who the heck is Garcia? That is not my job. Why don't you get Harry to do it? I don't have time. By the time you answer all the questions, you could have done the job yourself.

The individual who replies yes and then goes and does the task to the best of their ability is worth their weight in gold! That is the person you know you can depend on—one who can carry a message to Garcia. Like Nike says, just do it!

Initiative

On a previous show I was talking about carrying a message to Garcia. The story came from a marvelous book written by Elbert Hubbard in 1899 titled *A Message to Garcia*. Hubbard was a lecturer, publisher, editor, and essayist. He had a wonderful attitude toward work and wrote a number of essays that encourage us to enjoy our work and do a good job without being told. Permit me to share with you a real jewel he wrote on initiative.

"The world bestows its big prizes, both in money and honors, for but one thing, and that is Initiative.

"What is Initiative?

"I'll tell you: It is doing the right thing without being told.

"But next to doing the thing without being told is to do it when you are told once. That is to say, carry the Message to Garcia: those who can carry the message get high honors, but their pay is not always in proportion.

"Next, there are those who never do a thing until they are told twice; such get no honors and small pay.

"Next, there are those who do the right thing only when Necessity kicks them from behind, and these get indifference instead of honors, and a pittance for pay. This kind spends most of its time polishing a bench with a hard-luck story.

"Then, still lower down in the scale than this, we have the fellow who will not do the right thing even when someone goes along to show him how and stays to see that he does it: he is always out of a job, and receives the contempt he deserves, unless he happens to have a rich Pa, in which case Destiny patiently awaits around the corner with a stuffed club."

Well, that is how Elbert Hubbard saw the world and how it rewards those who do or do not apply themselves.

Initiative. Doing the right thing without being told. Remember that today and apply it in your business. Keep doing it every day until it becomes a habit. According to Hubbard, money and honors will be your reward.

Don't Become Complacent

If you are getting outstanding results, riding the crest of a wave of success is no guarantee of continued success. Many people have made such an error, and it has cost them dearly. They became complacent.

I can clearly remember when APECO, American Photo Copy Equipment Company, dominated the photocopy market. APECO was a giant; they were successfully selling their photocopiers in 152 countries. In fact, they were the first to bring a photocopier into the office environment—a piece of equipment that, today, is almost a necessity in every office.

Meanwhile a gentleman from Rochester, New York, was looking for a way to make a piece of equipment that would turn out a better copy. Because that is what Chester Carlson was looking for, that is exactly what he found. Today, everyone around the world recognizes Xerox, and hardly anyone remembers APECO because they have vanished.

The marketplace is very fickle. When someone presents a better or more efficient product, the people go with it. That's progress.

This was penned by the poet Braley:

> *For the best verse hasn't been rhymed yet.*
> *The best house hasn't been planned.*
> *The highest peak hasn't been climbed yet.*

The mightiest rivers aren't spanned.

Don't worry and fret, faint hearted.

The chances have just begun.

For the Best jobs haven't been started.

The Best work hasn't been done.

Invest a few minutes today and every day thinking of ways to do whatever you are doing better. You could be doing your job well. You might even be the best, but I can assure you there is always a Chester Carlson lurking in the wings. Keep doing what you did to win. Keep improving what you are doing.

The Conquest of Happiness

Studying the life of Bertrand Russell is like taking a mental ride on a roller coaster. He went from continually contemplating suicide as a boy to an extremely full life prior to his death in 1970 at the age of ninety-eight years. He was a professor at universities in China, Britain, and the United States.

He was imprisoned in both England and the United States for his outspoken views on religion, morals, sex, and leading movements to ban nuclear weapons. He had forty books published and earned a Nobel Prize for literature in 1950.

In his book *The Conquest of Happiness* published in 1930, Bertrand Russell shares an interesting lesson—a lesson perhaps you and I can benefit from. I quote:

"I was not born happy. As a child my favorite hymn was, 'Weary of earth and laden with sin.' ... In adolescence, I hated life and was continually on the verge of suicide, from which, however, I was restrained by the desire to know more mathematics. Now, on the contrary, I enjoy life; I might almost say that with every year that passes I enjoy it more ... very largely it is due to diminishing preoccupation with myself. Like others who had a Puritan education, I had a habit of meditating on my sins, follies, and shortcomings. I seemed to myself—no doubt justly—a miserable specimen.

"Gradually I learned to be indifferent to myself and my deficiencies; I came to center my attention increasingly upon external objects: the state of the world, various branches of knowledge, individuals for whom I felt affection."

I find that pretty interesting. His total disinterest with life and unhappy mental state was overcome when he ceased to be so self-centered. I believe the lesson for you and me is clear; to be happy, forget yourself and think of others.

Envy

In Ralph Waldo Emerson's essay on self-reliance he wrote that there would come a time in every person's education when they would realize that envy was ignorance.

Webster defines ignorance as lack of knowledge. Therefore, armed with the proper knowledge, envious individuals could eliminate a very destructive emotion from their lives and replace it with a magnificent awareness of the truth with respect to their own abilities. I am sure you would agree that the elimination of envy from a person's life would be nothing short of a tremendous rehabilitating experience.

The student who is failing may envy the honor student. The salesperson with low sales who works hard may envy the star. Athletes who never win may envy the athlete who earns the medals. Siblings may envy the success of other members of their own family. Frequently the person who gets the promotion is envied by his or her peers.

Envious people's unhappiness is caused by a lack of knowledge of their own potential. They have not learned the universal laws for a successful, well-balanced, fulfilled life.

The people who win follow the right rules. They have a better than average understanding of how their marvelous minds work with respect to the results they achieve. Winners are not swayed by the opinions of others or by the doom and gloom that will, from time to time, surround them.

People struggling with envy should realize they can build an image in their minds of the results they desire, and if they are true to those images, their desires must become a reality in their lives. We all have the same potential; how we use it is what makes us different.

Think Like a Winner

In a new book by Dr. Walter Staples, he opens with ten core beliefs that are unique to all peak performing men and women. In my opinion, it's a powerful and very accurate list. As you read the list, listen carefully and ask yourself, "Which of these core beliefs do I presently have fixed in my subconscious mind, and which of these beliefs should I work on?" Then pick one that needs improvement and begin to fix that belief deep within your mind for the next ninety days. It will change your life.

Here's the list:

1. **Winners are not born; they are made.**

2. **The dominant force in your existence is the thinking you engage in.**

3. **You are empowered to create your own reality.**

4. **There is some benefit to be had from every adversity.**

5. **Each one of your beliefs is a choice.**

6. **You are never defeated until you accept defeat as a reality and decide to stop trying.**

7. **You already possess the ability to excel in at least one key area of your life.**

8. **The only real limitations on what you can accomplish in your life are those you impose on yourself.**

9. There can be no great success without great commitment.

10. You need the support and cooperation of other people to achieve any worthwhile goal.

You can't help but win with a philosophy of life like that!

Your results are a direct reflection of the beliefs you hold. If you're unhappy with your results, simply change your beliefs. My favorite from this list is number three: you are empowered to create your own reality. Just think about it—you have the ability to create the type of world in which you'd like to live. Start creating your own reality today—live the way you choose!

Goals

A few years ago a young but excellent salesperson, Paul Kalia, gave me a cassette recording of a speech a minister out of Minneapolis had delivered to a sales convention in the United States. He said something in his speech I don't suppose I shall ever forget.

The minister said the saddest thing when he was officiating at a funeral was not the death of the body but the death of all the dreams.

Did he ever hit the nail on the head with that line! Think of the millions that go to their graves with the music still in them. They never had any goals.

It was the house they were going to build and never built or the business they were going to start, the car they longed to own, the trip they were going to take.

What do you want to be, do, or have? Make up your mind this very instant that you will accomplish it. Absolutely refuse to wait another day to begin working toward your goal.

James Allen in his wonderful little book *As a Man Thinketh* said, "Your circumstances may be uncongenial but they will not long remain so if you perceive an ideal and strive to reach it."

Forget about waiting until all your circumstances are favorable. Start right now. Begin by making a clearly defined written statement of your goal. Write your goal on a card and carry it with you and read it many times every day. This might sound like immature behavior, but believe me, it works for everyone who does it. This one act is what separates the poor from the rich, the weak from the strong, the sad from the happy. The most fulfilled human being is the one who is always pursuing meaningful goals.

Earn as Much as You Can

In Mark Victor Hansen's book *Dare to Win* (co-authored with Jack Canfield), he suggests that you, "Earn as much as you can, save as much as you can, invest as much as you can, give as much as you can."

You can have all that you want financially, and more. All it takes to achieve this is the proper state of mind. Prosperity is created by a state of mind. The principle is simple: get turned on about prosperity and stay turned on. Write down your prosperity goals, visualize them, affirm your prosperity regularly, and you'll achieve it.

It is better to have more than less. It is better to accumulate it more quickly rather than slowly. Money increases life's options. It creates new kinds of freedom and ends the slavery of poverty.

The question we all ask is, "How do we get it?" The answer is simple. Prosperity starts with an idea.

Mark writes, "Back in 1971, when I was launching my first business, I was in Boulder, Colorado. My friend Moe Siegel and I were full of wonderful buoyant energy. We'd go up and watch the sunset in what's called the flatirons of Boulder. Moe would always be picking seeds and herbs, and he would say, 'Someday I'll have a tea company to rival Lipton.' Everyone always said, 'Yeah, sure, sure.' Just a short time ago, Moe sold out for $105 million—net—to one of the biggest tea companies in the world. We all know his brand now as Celestial Seasonings."

Moe didn't start out with money. He started on the road to prosperity simply with an idea and the courage to believe in it.

Note from Author:

This story caught my eye with a smile. It references a book co-authored by Mark Victor Hansen and Jack Canfield. This was before both men authored *Chicken Soup for the Soul*. My wife Toni and I had the pleasure of spending a week with Mark Victor Hansen, Jack Canfield, Leland Val Van De Wall, my father, and many others when Mark and Jack were talking about their idea to write a book called *Chicken Soup for the Soul*. Look where that took them!

The Devil's Most Prized Possession

In a previous show I was talking about Earl Nightingale and the positive influence he had on my life. The personal association I had with him was a great education, but I could never estimate the effect his recorded messages have had on my life.

One of his recorded messages was titled "That's Good." I listened to it so often I could almost repeat it verbatim. On that record he shared a most interesting fable about the devil having a sale and, as Earl mentioned, like most old fables it has a moral that is worth thinking about.

The story goes that Satan was having a sale of his wares. There on display, and offered for sale, were the rapier of jealousy, the dagger of fear, and the strangling noose of hatred, each with its own high price.

But standing alone on a purple pedestal was a worn and battered wedge. This was the devil's most prized possession, for with it alone he could stay in business. It was not for sale—it was the wedge of discouragement.

Why do you suppose the devil valued so highly, and actually would not sell, the worn and battered wedge of discouragement? Makes you think doesn't it?

He prized discouragement because of its enfeebling, demoralizing effect. Hatred, fear, or jealousy may lead an immature person to act unwisely, to fight, or to run. But at least they act. Discouragement, on the other hand, hurts people more than any of these. It causes people to sit down, pity themselves, and do nothing.

Now this doesn't have to happen, but unfortunately it all too frequently does. Not until we realize that discouragement is often a form of self-pity, do we begin to take stock of ourselves and our predicament and decide to act—to do something that will take us out of the unpleasant situation.

The answer to discouragement then is intelligent action. Get rid of discouragement before it gets rid of you. The devil might not survive without this priceless wedge—but we can.

Discontented? Change It!

Anyone who reads a newspaper or tunes into the daily news would have to agree that there is a respectable amount of discontent with what is happening in our world. That observation applies locally, nationally, and internationally. Furthermore, the discontent we are experiencing deals with everything from taxes to transportation.

If you believe what most of us were programmed to believe as children, you would have to arrive at the conclusion this discontent was a negative force. However, if you have a close look at the history of all progress, you will realize discontent is a very positive, creative force. When everything in life is running smoothly, something most people long for, we have a tendency to become very satisfied and, quite often, complacent.

George Bernard Shaw said, "As long as I have a want, I have a reason for living. Satisfaction is death."

Thomas Alva Edison jarred our minds when he said, "Restlessness is discontent and discontent is the first necessity of progress. Show me a thoroughly satisfied person and I will show you a failure."

We should be careful not to confuse happiness with contentment, as there is a considerable difference.

It was Edison's discontent with the way in which we illuminated a darkened place that led us all to a better life. Discontentment has taken you and me out of the cave and put us in the condominium.

If you are discontented with what is happening in your world, don't sit back and complain. Let loose with your positive energy and change it—for the better!

You might not be able to change the situation you are discontented with internationally, but you most certainly can change your personal life.

Have More Fun

A delightful lady, Elizabeth Miner, was telling me about her recent family picnic. She said it seemed everything, including the weather, was perfect. When the picnic ended, one of her grandchildren began to cry, "I don't want to go home yet; we haven't had any fun!"

Elizabeth explained the child was probably right. Often everything can be running smoothly, but we don't have fun. She said we should have more fun.

Eighty-five-year-old Nadine Stair agreed. She said, "If I had my life to live over, I'd dare to make more mistakes next time. I'd relax. I would limber up. I would be sillier than I have been this trip. I would take fewer things seriously. I would take more chances. I would climb more mountains and swim more rivers. I would eat more ice cream and less beans. I would perhaps have more actual troubles, but I'd have fewer imaginary ones. You see, I'm one of those people who lives sensibly and sanely hour after hour, day after day. Oh, I've had my moments and if I had it to do over again, I'd have more of them. I've been one of those persons who never goes anywhere without a thermometer, a hot water bottle, a raincoat, and a parachute. If I had to do it again, I would travel lighter than I have. If I had my life to live over, I would start barefoot earlier in the spring and stay that way later into the fall. I would go to more dances. I would ride more merry-go-rounds. I would pick more daisies."

Giving

A good friend of mine, Dave Hynes, told me an interesting story. There are a couple of parts to this story, so you will have to bear with me.

Dave Hynes and Neil Burton recently attended one of my seminars. There is a part of the seminar that deals with giving—a basic rule if you want to enjoy abundance. We explained that your giving must be spontaneous or it is probably not giving at all; you are very likely trading.

Dave and Neil were recently at a business meeting. Another person at this meeting was admiring Neil Burton's leather jacket and said how he would truly love to have one like it. Neil promptly took the jacket off his back and gave it to the gentleman. Dave said he's never seen Neil happier. He truly enjoyed giving the jacket away.

Your immediate mental reaction could possibly be to think that Neil probably didn't like the jacket. I happened to have been in Spain at a conference with Neil Burton when he purchased this leather jacket. We both bought one, and I know for a fact he was quite fond of it.

Another lesson from the seminar on giving explains that if you are only giving away something you don't like or don't want, you will not likely benefit from your giving, as you are really just permitting someone to take away your garbage.

I can understand why Neil enjoyed his act of generosity, and you will as well by doing what Neil did.

If you want more love, give some away; more friends, be a friend; more money, give some away. This is a fundamental law of life. I believe we call it sowing and reaping.

Note from Author:

My first job out of university was selling insurance under Neil Burton's mentorship. He was a top producer at Prudential Assurance. When I think of Neil I think of his high energy in the office. He always moved forward saying "yah, yah" in a quick English accent. It was indicative of his "let's do it, it can be done" perspective.

Two Brush Strokes

"The Chinese use two brush strokes to write the word 'crisis.' One brush stroke stands for danger, the other for opportunity. In a crisis, be aware of the danger, but recognize the opportunity."

These words of Richard M. Nixon should be on your mind as you face each new crisis.

Among other things, crises represent opportunities to grow in wisdom. When you approach each crisis with this attitude, you will pluck the opportunity out of each situation and benefit from it. This attitude also sets the stage for you to continue to grow mentally.

Everyone has problems and the real producers have crises. Former President Richard Nixon certainly had his. He must be an authority on the subject, and he is also an authority on opportunity.

Richard Nixon has wisdom and mental strength. He wasn't born with these qualities; he developed them. All great leaders do. The important element is how you handle crises.

Most public personalities must be mental giants. Their lives are examined and openly criticized frequently. For many people this would be an unbearable crisis. However, to the personality that has high goals and a strong desire to reach them, the public criticism is viewed as unpleasant but a necessary part of gaining experience.

A diamond in its original state is a rough piece of coal It is only through extreme pressure that it becomes a beautiful gem.

"Crisis" has two brush strokes. One stands for danger, the other for opportunity. Be aware of danger, but recognize the opportunity. Excellent advice; don't shy away from a crisis. You will become a stronger person from it.

Forget Yourself

If you happen to be attracting an inordinate amount of personal problems, there is probably a fairly simple solution to your predicament. Forget yourself! That may sound strange, but it will probably work. Forget yourself!

You might be asking, How do I do that? Try thinking about someone else who has greater need than yourself and get busy helping that person.

The late Bill Wilson found this worked wonders for him close to sixty years ago. He believed his situation to be hopeless. Bill Wilson was a very sick alcoholic and was experiencing all of the problems that normally accompany someone in his state. He found someone who was in as bad, if not worse, shape than himself and helped him. Together they gave birth to Alcoholics Anonymous.

The underlying principle of their organization is simple—help someone else. It works. Their basic concept has been copied by numerous other groups of people who are experiencing personal problems. When people have personal problems, they seem to focus all of their attention on themselves and their problems. That attitude will cause any situation to grow—even bad situations.

John Ruskin expressed it another way: "When a person is wrapped up in himself, he makes a pretty small package."

I have found through personal experience that this idea of helping others first works. I have a good friend, Og Mandino, who has become a world-famous author and has helped millions of people. He was down and out, alone and lonely because he was focusing on himself and his problems. Og switched his thinking and began giving his attention to helping others. His reward is fame and fortune.

Eliminate your problems by forgetting yourself and get busy helping others.

Attraction

Have you ever spent time wondering why some people continually attract negative situations into their lives, while others seem to attract nothing but beautiful situations into theirs? The concept behind this "Law of Attraction" contains power, possibility, and promise if you will use it.

You are a living, breathing, creative magnet. You have the ability to control what you attract into your life. Why not make a conscious decision to attract into your life all of the good you desire. Historically, there have always been small, select groups of individuals who were aware of how to work in harmony with this natural law of the universe.

The Law of Attraction

This law clearly states, you can only attract to you that which is in harmony with you. Everything in this universe vibrates, including your mind and body. Look at your body through a microscope. It is a mass of energy—moving, vibrating.

Your mind controls the vibration you are in at any given moment. You control your mind by the thoughts you choose. No one can cause you to think something you don't want to think. This is where freedom comes in. This is also where the problem begins with most people. They permit what is happening around them to determine how they think.

Ninety percent of the population wish positive but think negative. Their negative thoughts put them in a negative vibration, which, by law, determines what is attracted into their lives. As a creative individual, you will continually attract good things into your life by thinking positive thoughts and expecting the best life has to offer. You deserve it.

Note from Author:

My father's knowledge on the subject of the Law of Attraction has clearly made him famous through the bestselling movie and book *The Secret*.

Do Little Things in a Big Way

John Kanary is a good friend and business associate of mine. He and I have worked together for years and have often shared the stage when conducting seminars in various parts of the world. A few weeks ago, I was reading something John had written and decided I would share it with you. John was writing about talented people who fail and others who appear quite ordinary but are extremely successful.

Quite often very talented people fail because they believe they are too big to do the little things, while the most successful among us are quite willing to do the little things. They truly are big people.

John went on to explain how a successful, balanced life is comprised of a lot of successful days put together, and each day is made up of a lot of successful activities, each activity completed in an extraordinary way. Our lives are made up of many small parts, and we should capitalize on small victories, recognizing that extraordinary achievements come from people who are often considered to be very ordinary.

Realize that nobody is ordinary; every person is extraordinary.

Here are a few simple rules that John suggests and any person can follow:

1. **Stop thinking of yourself as ordinary.**

2. Never refer to yourself as an average person because there are no average people. Our problems stem from acting as though we are average.

3. Consider every person a very important person. Dispense with the status quo in your personal and business life.

4. Develop the attitude that there are no small parts in the movie of life; there are only small actors.

5. Do the smallest of jobs in the best way you possibly can.

6. Organize your small victory list every day and make them all important activities. Complete each one enthusiastically.

Everyone expects us to have a sense of urgency for life's big things. Life measures us by how we engage ourselves in the little things.

The Imagi-nation

There are very few people who have disciplined themselves to think in an orderly way—creatively and with some continuity. The majority spend their time reviewing past events, holding on especially to the unpleasant and disturbing things that have come their way. They allow impressions of their surroundings to govern their lives, and once in a while, for variety, they contemplate the future by either worrying about it or daydreaming and wishing that something better would come along. They apparently have never been taught the value of creative vision and purposeful thinking.

If you doubt me, just try listening to the varied conversations that are going on around you today. What you will hear is an orgy of disconnected thoughts with very little effort put forth to carry on a purposeful conversation. While it is true that people are free to think anything they please, as long as they are satisfied and set in their ways there is very little that can be done to change the unpleasant experiences that keep cropping up in their lives.

There is, however, a strong movement that is stirring the multitudes into a new conception of living, and the study of the mind is taking its proper place in modern civilization. Proper use of the mind will give you anything you choose—but you must use it and use it properly. This requires study.

In the classic movie, *Miracle on 34th Street*, Kris Kringle tells young Susie Walker she can become whatever she chooses through the aid of her imagination. Kris goes on to explain that the Imagi-nation is a place we can all go visit, just like the British nation or the French nation.

Go to the Imagi-nation and reshape your life.

Imagi-nation Part Two

Looking at the Imagi-nation as a place we can all go to, like the British nation or the French nation, is a cute and healthy way to remember your ability to use the imagination any time you want. It is a place you can visit in your mind. Free will is your passport. No one is ever refused entry. There are no borders or limits put on the size of what can be built. It is a universal nation in which we are all citizens. What Kris told Susie is true for you and me. We can be, do, and have whatever we choose.

Your future should be looked at with intelligence, anticipated with imagination, and designed with care.

Go to that mental nation and build a beautiful picture of where you want to find yourself one year from today.

Your mental growth or development will determine what the future has in store for you. Design an effective program for your own personal development. Build a worthwhile library. Make a list of twelve good books you will read and refer to, one each month. Select four excellent seminars you will attend, one every quarter—seminars that will help you understand the awesome powers you possess and how to utilize those powers in a practical way to improve the quality of your life. Play motivational audio recordings; turn your car into a learning center.

Commit to reaching your goal. The only thing separating you from the goal is ignorance—replace the ignorance with knowledge.

Age Is No Excuse

There are literally thousands of people who deny themselves an exciting life because of their age. They fail to act on their big idea because they think they are either too young or too old.

Sad, isn't it? Especially when you consider that life is much like a dollar bill: once you have spent it, you cannot spend it again. Thoroughly enjoy your life and don't permit age to hold you back. Age has very little, if anything, to do with ability.

Do something—something you have always wanted to do. Start your own business; build your dream house; take that trip and forget your age.

Colonel Saunders started Kentucky Fried Chicken with his first social security check. Look at it today.

Golda Meir was seventy-one when she became prime minister of Israel.

Benjamin Franklin was a newspaper columnist at sixteen and a framer of the United States Constitution at eighty-one.

George Bernard Shaw was ninety-four when one of his plays was first produced.

William Pitt II was twenty-four when he became prime minister of Great Britain.

Mozart was just seven when his first composition was published.

How old would you be if you forgot your age? That might be a good question to ask yourself every now and then. If you have been using age as an excuse in the past, make up your mind this very moment to change.

What do you want to do? What is something you have always wanted to do? Go for it!

Start right now and don't worry about what *they* will say. What *they* are saying should have no bearing on your decision.

If you have been using age as an excuse, let this moment be the trigger to fire you down the road to a bright future.

Kindness

There are some people who say this is a hard, tough world and that kindness might be all right for a Sunday school picnic, but has no place in business. If you're ever going to get anywhere, you have to be hardboiled. Not so; kindness works everywhere.

Years ago in Philadelphia, a couple walked into a hotel. There was a big convention in the city and no vacant rooms available. They asked the clerk for a room, but he told them they were booked. This clerk believed in kindness and, noticing how tired the couple was, he said they could use his room for the night. It was small and unpretentious, but if they wanted it, he would sleep in the lobby. He assured them he was young and one night in the lobby wouldn't hurt him.

The next morning the man sought out the young clerk. He told him how much he appreciated his spirit and that he had what it took to go far. Then he said, "If you will allow me, I want to build for you the greatest hotel ever erected in America."

The man was Mr. Astor, and he built the old Waldorf Astoria Hotel. The clerk was George C. Boldt, who managed the Waldorf Astoria and became one of the greatest hotel men in America.

Kindness is a positive thing. It's something we must think about and cultivate. All too often, we forget the things we should remember; we do not weigh our words before we speak, and we allow our moods to control our actions. I know of nothing that opens the doors of opportunity and wins friends as quickly and as effectively as kindness does.

You never know when you're being kind to a Mr. Astor!

Ls / Mft

Many years ago a tobacco company had a famous radio commercial. If you are old enough, you remember the magic letters LS/MFT that were used in that commercial.

Les Giblin in his book *How to Have Confidence and Power in Dealing with People*, gives new meaning to those magic letters. Giblin suggests that LS/MFT represents "low self-esteem means friction and trouble." I agree with him, and you will as well when you think about it. The higher a person's self-esteem, the easier the person is to deal with. These people are cheerful, generous, tolerant, and willing to listen to people's ideas. Their personalities are well-developed; they are mentally strong and capable of taking a risk. They can afford to be wrong on occasion and are not afraid to admit it. They take criticism in their stride as it only makes a small dent in their self-esteem and they have plenty more left. The person at the top is always easier to deal with.

Here is a magic rule you would be wise to remember. Listen closely. Never, never offend a person with low self-esteem in a position of authority. It could prove to be costly.

There is a wonderful story about a private in World War I who shouted, "Put out that damn match." He then realized he was shouting at General Black Jack Pershing. As the private began to sputter and stutter out an apology, the good general gave the young private a pat on the back and said, "It's OK son, don't worry about it. Just be thankful that I wasn't a second lieutenant."

When a person's self-esteem is low, friction and trouble come easy. There is a great lesson here for everyone. Remember, LS/MFT.

Thinking

Many years ago I was attending a seminar that a good friend of mine was conducting. He said something that broke me up; in fact, the entire audience roared with laughter. He said, "If most people said what they were thinking, they would be speechless." Statements such as that roll out of Val Van De Wall; he is a very wise man. He is correct as well.

A number of years ago I had the pleasure of sharing the platform at a convention with the late Dr. Kenneth MacFarland, a great educator from Kentucky. He said something similar. Dr. MacFarland said, "Two percent of the people think, 3 percent think they think, and 95 percent would rather die than think."

I recently read where George Bernard Shaw said, "Most people think two or three times a year. I've gained an international reputation for myself thinking just two or three times a week."

You are probably saying to yourself by now, come on Bob, everyone thinks. Is that right? Well let me suggest that you listen closely to most of the conversations going on around you over the next few hours. It will be obvious most of those talking are not thinking, or they would never say what they are saying.

Watch the behavior of some of your peers. You will realize they are not thinking, or they would never do what they are doing.

You could fall into the 3 percent group, which Dr. MacFarland referred to as those who think they think. With a little effort you could catapult yourself into the 2 percent group that does think. They are the achievers, the winners in life.

Thinking must be learned, and it is a subject not taught in most schools. Think about it.

Acceptance

There are a number of people who cheat themselves out of a lot of good days. They put themselves into a poor frame of mind by judging others, criticizing people, or looking for the faults of others. Here is an idea that will almost guarantee you a good day, every day. I can almost see the smile on your face waiting to hear this. It's true! Use this idea and you'll have a great day.

Accept everyone you meet. Sounds simple enough doesn't it? But, hold on a minute … there is more to it. Accept them just as they are. Don't try to change them … that will probably require a little more effort.

A leading psychologist once suggested, "No one has the power to reform another person, but by liking the other person as he is, you give him the power to change himself." Pretty interesting isn't it?

Here's another psychologist's view on the same subject. "If people really practiced acceptance, we'd soon be out of business. For the very heart of psychoanalysis is that the patient finds one person - the doctor - who will accept him. For the first time in his life, he lets his hair down, he brings out his fears, the things he is ashamed of, and the doctor listens without surprise or horror or moral judgement. Because he has found one human being who shows acceptance in spite of all his shameful traits and faults, he is able to accept himself and then he is on the road to better living."

You don't have to be a psychologist or an analyst to be a big help to others by doing what the doctor does. Just listen ... don't judge ... accept the other person.

Try it today!

Personal Power

I once heard it said that the world will forgive you if you make mistakes, but that life will not forgive you if you fail to make decisions.

With all the material that has been written on the subject of personal power, I seldom hear that decision-making is the first principle in the development of your personal power.

The fear of making a decision is the result of fearing to make a mistake and, as Huxley once wrote, "The fear of mistakes has a greater impact on you than making the mistakes."

Now would be a good time for you to get a notepad and write down three areas that affect you daily:

1. **Where you are**

2. **Where you want to be**

3. **The steps needed to bridge the gap**

This process will put you face-to-face with decisions you must make. As with every decision, there is the worst that could happen to you and the best that could happen to you. Write each side down and ask yourself what you would do if the worst happened and then think of how much more beautiful life would be when the best happens.

This method by no means eliminates the risk you must take, but it does generate a more prepared mind and a more productive attitude for action. It also helps you become aware of some of the obstacles you must eliminate.

A study made of the lives of thousands of highly successful people showed that they all made decisions quickly and changed them very slowly, if they changed them at all.

Your personal power is moved into action by decision.

Smiles

Since time began we have been told by the wise that giving is much more beneficial than receiving. There have probably been many occasions when you had a good reason to question that advice, but even in those moments your higher self would probably agree with the concept. I came across something in a file I keep that suggests there is something you can give every day, and it will provide you with great compensation.

"It costs nothing, but creates much. It enriches those who receive, without impoverishing those who give. It happens in a flash and the memory of it sometimes lasts forever.

"None are so rich that they can get along without it, and none are so poor but are richer for its benefits. It creates happiness in the home, fosters good will in a business and is the countersign of friends. Your gift will provide rest for the weary, daylight to the discouraged, sunshine to the sad and nature's best antidote for trouble.

"Yet, it cannot be bought, begged, borrowed, or stolen for it is something that is no earthly good to anybody till it is given away! And, if it ever happens that a salesperson should be too tired to give one of these to you, you may want to give them one of yours.

"For nobody needs one of these so much as those who have none left to give."

This is a bit of a riddle isn't it? What on earth could provide so much for so little?

A *smile*—that's right, a smile.

Make up your mind to give a big one to every person you come in contact with today.

A smile … from ear to ear, and pay particular attention to the reaction you get from every person you give one to. Professionals who train people on the proper use of the telephone will tell you to smile when you are using the telephone and it will improve your effectiveness.

Imagineering

Every company has a Randy Hayden. If they don't have one, they should. Randy is the person in our company that could very easily lead you to believe he ate a dictionary as a child. If ever I am stuck for a word, I know where to find it.

The other day Randy tossed out a word and asked me if I was familiar with it. Oddly enough I was … it is imagineering. I first became familiar with imagineering many years ago. It came from a program produced by Earl Nightingale on creative thinking.

Imagineering is a wonderful way to solve problems, to come up with new ways to sell your product or service—a great concept to assist you in reaching your goals. I've often felt if we were really on our toes, we would have imagineering as part of the curriculum in school as we do with engineering. Unfortunately, when our youngsters in school get involved with imagineering, they are frequently chastised for daydreaming.

Try it. Get off in a quiet place by yourself or with other open-minded individuals. Write out a problem you may want to solve or an objective you would like to accomplish. Then let your imagination run wild. Let it soar—no-limit thinking. There are no foolish ideas; there are only ideas. As these ideas come to you, jot them down, then go in search of a new idea and jot it down.

You will find imagineering can be fun. It is invigorating. New energy will suddenly fill every fiber of your being. Most of us are stuck in conditioned habitual ways of doing whatever we are doing. Imagineering will prove to be a refreshing change for you.

Note from Author:

Randy Hayden has been a close friend of our family for a couple of decades. He has an incredible talent for making you feel special and appreciated just by the way he says "Hello" to you.

Paralyze Resistance

Albert Einstein once said, "Great spirits have always encountered violent opposition from mediocre minds." Actually, there is no such thing as a mediocre mind. The mind is the greatest power in all of creation. There are only people who use the awesome power of their mind for mediocre purposes, and, unfortunately, when some great spirit surfaces to do great deeds, those same small-thinking individuals violently oppose them rather than joining in and elevating their own lives.

These great spirits Einstein was referring to are often considered radicals or dreamers. They are seldom taken seriously by those individuals who seem to be satisfied with the status quo. For years I lived in that humdrum state myself, so I have some appreciation for their view of the world.

Thirty years ago I made a decision to change my way of thinking. Today I live a vastly different life. My associates and I are presently setting up a worldwide distribution system of good development programs. We are already in a number of different countries. Tomorrow I leave for India and Malaysia. It is a big idea and we have attracted many great people to work on this with us. But, believe me, we have also encountered violent opposition on numerous fronts.

The other day I came across a line by John Ruskin that anyone who is working with a big idea can use. Ruskin said we could, "paralyze resistance with persistence."

If you are working on a big idea, you will very likely encounter more opposition than acceptance. Only those who work with big ideas are capable of even thinking about yours. Understand why people oppose you and follow Ruskin's advice, and "paralyze resistance with persistence."

Commitment to Your Goal

Today our focus is on a salesperson's commitment to his or her goal. A salesperson without a goal is automatically disqualified as a professional. However, merely setting a goal is not sufficient. You must make that all-important mental connection to your goal that is referred to as commitment. That is when you make a conscious decision that regardless of how many roadblocks or detours you encounter as you move toward your goal, you will keep on keeping on. The goal must be reached. If your goal is a big one, you are going to encounter problems, and you will have to be strong to overcome them.

Every project has, within it, an escape hatch and if you are not committed to getting the job done, you will hit the escape hatch and never realize what you were capable of doing.

The amateur is not committed to a goal; in fact, the average amateur never had a goal to pursue in the first place.

When amateurs hit the escape hatch and settle for failure, they very rarely, if ever, blame themselves. The saddest thing about quitting is that every time a salesperson quits, he or she has made it just a little easier to do the same thing the next time the going gets tough, which it inevitably will.

The beautiful part about being committed to your goal is that every time you press on and go over the hurdle, it becomes easier for you to handle the next problem when it comes along. You eventually form the habit of winning.

Make a binding commitment to your goal. It will virtually blind you from many of the small annoyances that would otherwise distract and confuse you.

125

Affirmations

Affirmations are power statements that stimulate your mind and add a dimension to your life. If you are wondering where to get them, look no further than yourself. You originate them.

Quite often affirmations are referred to as auto-suggestion or self-talk. Affirmations are positive statements that, when given to your subconscious mind repetitively, have a tendency to alter old habits or old conditioning.

Napoleon Hill in his masterpiece *Think and Grow Rich* refers to auto-suggestions as the "third step toward riches." He felt this was such an important subject that he dedicated the entire fourth chapter of his book to auto-suggestion or affirmation. Hill explained that affirmation is the agency of communication between the part of the mind where conscious thought takes place and that which serves as the seat of action for the subconscious mind.

The great poets and philosophers of the past have all told us many times that you and I can control our destinies. However, they neglected to explain how.

1. **Decide what you want.**

2. **Make a written statement indicating you are already in possession of this.**

3. **Repeat the statement aloud many times every day with a strong feeling of gratitude.**

4. **Then expect the materialization of your desire in your physical world.**

By repeating the statement in the present tense with strong feeling, you are depositing an image of prosperity in the treasury of your subconscious mind. The subconscious does all the work with and through you. Your present results are the reflection of your subconscious. James Allen wrote, "You think in secret and it comes to pass. Environment is but your looking glass."

Affirmations ... try them.

Can

Possibly the most aggravating or the most motivating words you will ever hear as you begin what appears to be a very difficult task are the words, "It can't be done."

The Wright Brothers heard them prior to introducing us to a new kingdom. Bill Lear heard them when he was planning to build his jet airplane. Roger Bannister heard them prior to breaking the four-minute mile record. And, Thomas Edison must have heard them frequently before he illuminated the world.

Read this poem carefully. It is a classic titled "It Can't Be Done."

> *The man who misses all the fun*
> *Is he who says, "It can't be done."*
> *In solemn pride, he stands aloof*
> *And greets each venture with reproof.*
>
> *Had he the power, he would efface*
> *The history of the human race.*
> *We'd have no steam or trolley cars,*
> *No streets lit by electric stars.*
>
> *No telegraph or telephone,*
> *We'd linger in the age of stone*

Where when some keen barbaric brain.

Of life's conditions dared complain.

And planned a wheel on which to roll

The load his arms could not control.

Sneers arise from all the crew

That ever scoffs at which is new.

The world would sleep if things were run

By men who say, "It can't be done."

Isn't that a beauty. Get a copy and give it out at work. The next time you catch yourself using those words, correct yourself by saying, "I don't know how, but I can." If you want to do it, learn how.

Getting Life's Answers

I recently prepared a program on mastering whatever you do, which of course requires endless study and continuous effort. Shortly after writing the program, I read these verses written by J. M. Robertson. I enjoyed them—probably because I related to his message. You might as well.

I thought I knew the answers, when I was 17.

And simply couldn't wait to grace

The intellectual scene.

I thought I knew the answers, when I was 21.

But found that all life's question marks,

Had only just begun.

I thought I knew the answers, when I was 33.

Yet soon discovered Fate had played

Some funny tricks on me.

I thought I knew the answers, but hastened to recall,

As time went by, it seemed that I

Just didn't know 'em all.

Now I'm 59, I think it's fairly safe to say,

Experience can help, but still

I'm learning every day.

Mr. Robertson and I are not too far apart in age, and, judging from his writing, we are close in awareness as well.

If you are seventeen, twenty-one, or thirty-three and can grasp the importance of Robertson's advice, you will not only save yourself from numerous heartaches, you will be a happier, healthier, and more prosperous person. I have found that learning is a lifelong process, and you and I can benefit from the experience and wisdom of others.

Henry Drummond said that, through their writings, we can learn from people who have been dead for a couple of thousand years. If you don't have a well-stocked library of good books, begin to build one. Realize that there are tremendous benefits to be had by encountering the minds of great authors.

Study

A clear 90 percent of the population in North America reads at a Grade seven level. That's because we learn to read by the time we have reached Grade seven and never improve our reading ability from that point on. Shocking isn't it?

It is not only shocking, it's a shame. But what is even worse is that this lack of personal development goes well beyond reading. Most people do whatever they do in much the same manner. There are very few people who master anything. Ask a few sales executives, and they will quickly agree there are mighty few people who ever master selling. The same is true of managers, lawyers, accountants … I could go on.

There is really no competition in the marketplace. You'll have great masses in any profession out there making noise. Those few souls who are actually studying their craft, attempting to perfect it, stand out in a crowd like a giraffe in a flock of sheep.

The masters in any profession can name their own price, write their own ticket. Yes, their stock is always high; their rewards are great. If you don't already belong to this small select group of high achievers, I have good news. There is plenty of room in their club, and it is not difficult to qualify.

Begin to study what you do for a short time every day, knowing you can always perform better. Work toward a specific result well beyond your present level of performance.

Just one hour of concentrated study each day adds up to nine, forty-hour weeks in one short year. Think of how much more you would know in five, ten, or twenty years.

I began doing this myself twenty-five years ago. Today, I receive more money for one hour of my time than what I was once paid annually. When I started to study, I learned this great secret of achievement. If you want more, you must know more; to know more, you must study.

Earn a Million

There is a tremendous mass of evidence to prove that an imaginative, resourceful, and dynamic person has more opportunities to achieve wealth and success in business today than ever before in our history. Countless alert and aggressive people have proved this by making their fortunes in a wide variety of business endeavors in recent years. Contrary to popular modern belief, it is still quite possible to earn a million. The door to the "millionaire's club" is certainly not locked.

Don't build your hopes too high … be careful … you have to be realistic … you're too young. This is the negative advice offered by supposedly intelligent people. If you want to accomplish something—accomplish anything—go to a person who has done it; they know.

Last month in our Goal Achiever Seminar there was a young man who wanted to set the goal of owning his own home. He wasn't going to set the goal until he found a better job though. I introduced him to a friend of mine who was sitting directly behind the young man. This gentleman didn't even have a job, yet he owned nine houses, and, until five years ago, he had no money and no houses.

How he did all of this is another story. The fact is that he did it, and he is worth a couple of million dollars today. I suggested the young man spend some time talking with my friend.

There is a formula for success, and the door to the "millionaire's club" is not locked! However, a definite goal and an "I can" attitude are essential if you want to accomplish material wealth. The formula for success is not difficult; anyone can learn it, but rest assured, success is no accident.

Build a Cathedral

Three bricklayers were interrupted and asked what they were doing. "Laying bricks," replied the first. "Earning a living," replied the second. "Building a great cathedral," said the third man.

Of the three, the third person is the only one who was more than a bricklayer. The first two people have very little chance of progress, while the third has his mind focused on doing something of importance with his life.

It's not their skill or knowledge, but the awareness of what they are doing and why they are doing it that separates one from another.

It is interesting to notice how much more a person gets out of a job when it is approached as a very special project filled with meaning.

How you spend your days and the attitude with which you approach your work are vitally important to your unfoldment as a creative being. You have the ability to add meaning to whatever you may be doing today. Put your heart and soul into every task at hand; then watch your work come alive.

There is another very good reason for approaching your work with an attitude like the bricklayer who was building a great cathedral. You will never be paid for more than you are doing if you are not prepared to do more than you are being paid for.

Straight A's

In school, straight A's were always indicative of a great year. In business, the same rule applies—straight A's will give you what you want every time. With Awareness, Acceptance, and Alteration comes Achievement.

First you must become Aware of the primary cause of the results you are getting. The truth is not always in the appearance of things. Your results are never caused by something outside of yourself; results are always an inside job. Your results are a physical or outward expression of the inner conditioning in your subconscious mind. Your behavior is causing your results … and your conditioning is causing your behavior.

The second A is Acceptance. You must accept responsibility for your results. When you accept full responsibility for your own results, you will make the necessary decisions to alter them. Acceptance of this truth is always the preamble to a magnificent future.

When you accept your subconscious conditioning as the cause of your results, you will be ready for the third A—Alteration. You must decide to alter the conditioning in your subconscious mind, conditioning that is both genetic and environmental. You and your results are actually the product of someone else's habitual way of thinking. To make the necessary alterations in this area not only takes time, it takes a respectable amount of study and discipline, but it's worth it. It is well worth every penny and every speck of energy you invest in learning how to alter your old conditioning. This simple process will permit you to Achieve whatever goal you set.

Let's review it. Become aware of the cause of your results. Accept responsibility for your results. Alter your conditioned subconscious mind. Achieve any goal you set. Straight A's.

What Do You Think?

Do you ever give much consideration to your own thoughts? What are thoughts? How do they affect the various aspects of your life? Although this should be one of our most serious considerations, unfortunately, for many people it is not. If the truth were known, there is a very small select few who make any attempt to govern their thoughts.

Anyone who has made a study of the great thinkers, the great writers, or achievers of history, knows they very rarely agreed on anything when it came to a study of human life. However, there was one point on which they were in complete agreement, and that one point was, of course, that we become what we think about. What do you think about?

The majority of people you are surrounded by permit their thinking to be controlled by what is happening around them. Their world is in control of them; they are not in control of their world. If you doubt this, pay particular attention to the behavior and conversations of the people you come in contact with today. You will quickly see that these people are reacting to their environment, rather than originating positive, constructive thoughts and then acting upon them.

You and I must realize that our thoughts ultimately control everything we have or do. You are the sum total of your thoughts. By taking charge this very minute, you can guarantee yourself a good day regardless of what happens. Refuse to let unhappy, negative people affect how you see them. Look for and think of what is good. There is good in everyone and everything. These are just a few thoughts for you to think about today.

They should then continue doing what they have already been doing with a part of every day even if it is only a small part and educate themselves.

Thirty minutes of concentrated study each day adds up to four and a half forty-hour weeks each year. Any sales manager will tell you that that amount of time devoted to simulating a sales presentation each day will make a star out of any young salesperson. The same applies to any profession.

You may be leaving school, but never stop learning.

Continuing Education

My son, Raymond, graduates from university next month. Some of his comments over the past couple of months have been priceless. The other day he phoned home, and, during our conversation, he said he felt like his brain had been fried from so many years of studying.

It is my opinion that Raymond and his fellow students who are graduating are in for a reality shock treatment when they enter the free market place. Their education is just beginning.

The term "continuing education" is relatively new. However, anyone who hopes to survive and prosper in the fast lane must never cease learning. We are all in the fast lane today, whether we like it or not.

Education, or learning, must become a part of our everyday diet. These are the golden years we have been waiting for ... working for ... looking for ... for centuries.

The conveniences that are at our fingertips today would have seemed inconceivable a short time ago, but there is a price to be paid. We must continue our education.

The people who ignore this fact will be left behind, and their lot will not be a pretty one. The achievers are those individuals who are forever learning more about their wonderful self and their business and/or industry.

The graduating students would be wise to make a mental note of just how important learning is to their future well-being.

Dad and I on Graduation Day.

The Conquest Of Happiness

Studying the life of Bertrand Russell is like taking a mental ride on a roller-coaster. He went from continually contemplating suicide as a boy to an extremely full life prior to his death in 1970 at the age of 98 years. He was a professor at universities in China, Britain and the United States.

He was imprisoned in both England and the United States for his outspoken views on religion, morals, sex, and leading movements to ban nuclear weapons. He had 40 books published and earned a Nobel Prize for literature in 1950.

In his book *The Conquest for Happiness,* published in 1930, Bertrand Russell shares an interesting lesson ... a lesson perhaps you and I can benefit from. I quote:

"I was not born happy. As a child my favorite hymn was, 'Weary of earth and laden with sin...' in adolescence, I hated life and was continually on the verge of suicide, from which, however, I was restrained by the desire to know more mathematics. Now, on the contrary, I enjoy life; I might almost say that with every year that passes I enjoy it more... very largely it is due to diminishing preoccupation with myself. Like others who had a Puritan education, I had a habit of meditating on my sins, follies and shortcomings. I seemed to myself ... no doubt justly ... a miserable specimen.

"Gradually I learned to be indifferent to myself and my deficiencies: I came to center my attention upon external objects; the state of the world, various branches of knowledge, individuals for whom I felt affection."

I find that pretty interesting. His total disinterest with life and unhappy mental state was overcome when he ceased to be so self centered. I believe the lesson for you and I is clear, to be happy, forget yourself and think of others.

Walls

One evening I sat comfortably in our den with a log burning in the fireplace. I was watching the late news on television from West Germany. Thousands of East Germans were streaming into the West, excited about their new freedom. One person was purchasing fresh oranges; another was buying a small battery-operated toy. These were gifts they were taking back to loved ones who had remained in the East.

Many of the reports were about simple, everyday activities, which most of us who enjoy our freedom take for granted. However, they were not simple everyday activities to these East Germans; they were new, first-time experiences to some of these individuals. They had been living in an enormous prison surrounded by a concrete wall, manned by armed guards who had been ordered to shoot anyone who dared to wander into the West, even if they were only in search of a fresh orange or small toy.

It's wonderful to see a wall coming down. The doors to the prison are once again open.

Watching these reports I thought about the prisons many of us put ourselves in, the imaginary walls we build, which confine our movements. These imaginary walls are every bit as real and confining in the mind of the person who built them as the Berlin Wall.

Vernon Howard wrote that you cannot escape from a prison if you do not know you are in one. Everyone has their own

Berlin Wall, but it does not have armed guards, and the wall will disappear when we tell it to. The walls that confine us are limitations.

Let's begin to think, to see doors instead of walls. Then we will truly enjoy the freedom that is our birthright.

The Sisters Are Doctors

I love success stories and here is a beauty! It comes from Julie Morris written for *USA Today*.

They are $80,000 in debt from school loans and face four years of grueling training, but Huong and Trang Le, refugees 14 years ago, will become doctors next week.

"When we came to the United States our goal was the education of our children," says Dr. Lan Le an anesthesiologist from Dallas. We express our gratitude to all the people who helped us, he said. Huong 26, and Trang 24, say future careers were the last thing on their minds when they fled South Vietnam in 1975, a week before the last U.S. citizens were evacuated from the country.

"We packed everything in two suitcases. We just took off. We were so grateful just not to be killed," says Huong. She remembers almost 100 people being crammed into a helicopter meant for 75. No one spoke after takeoff from Saigon.

Five months later, sponsored by a church, the family was resettled in Baytown, Texas. When Huong and Trang started school, they were the only Vietnamese in class and they spoke no English. The family later moved to Worcester, Massachusetts. In Worcester, both Huong and Trang were high school valedictorians, student government officers and editors on the school paper. They became U.S. citizens in 1981.

Both enrolled in Houston's Baylor College of Medicine after graduating from Rice University in Houston. Both married doctors in the past year. But now they are going their separate ways. Trang who plans to be an ophthalmologist, will intern at Baylor and the University of Arizona in Tucson. Huong plans a career as a family physician, and will intern at a county hospital in Conroe, Texas.

It's stories such as this that inspire us. Individuals like Huong and Trang set a beautiful example for others. And, like many others who have become great achievers, these ladies were forced into situations that, to many, would have been devastating.

Realize the problems you face today are probably small by comparison to those Huong and Trang faced, but they persisted by focusing on a goal. Follow their example today and do likewise.

Simple Rules

Do you sometimes think that we often complicate our lives, when, by following a few simple rules we could relax, have fun, and probably be just as productive, possibly more productive than we are?

The beautiful truth is that 99 percent of us had the very basic rules for a happy, productive, fulfilling life programmed into our minds as children. As we get a little older, our ego probably gets in the way, and many of these good rules are put on the back burner. Unfortunately, they are too often forgotten completely.

Robert Fulghum wrote a book that will raise the spirits and warm the heart: *All I Really Need to Know I Learned in Kindergarten.* His book has a magic attached to it that could very easily turn it into a modern classic. Fulghum wrote about those wonderful rules we were freely given as little children.

Here are some of those rules he learned and writes about: "Share everything. Play fair. Don't hit people. Put things back where you found them. Clean up your mess. Don't take things that aren't yours. Say you're sorry when you hurt somebody. Wash your hands before you eat. Flush. Warm cookies and cold milk are good for you. Live a balanced life—learn some and think some, and draw and paint and sing and dance, and play and work every day.... When you go out into the world, watch out for traffic, hold hands and stick together. Be aware of wonder."

If Robert Fulghum's rules sound too trite, too simple to give serious thought to, think about them again. I recommend his book to anyone who is in search of a more prosperous and happy life. It is fun reading, and you will pick up many marvelous ideas!

Chatter of the Masses

Reader's Digest is a great publication. It always has a number of articles that are mentally stimulating. The following lines were picked up from a *Reader's Digest* a number of years ago.

> *Small minds talk about people.*
>
> *Average minds talk about events.*
>
> *Great minds talk about ideas.*

I have come to believe this is fairly accurate. I suppose we all fall into the first two categories—talking about people and events—periodically. However, have you ever noticed that those two categories dominate the conversation of most people? Listen carefully and you will hear a buzz of meaningless noise going on around you almost constantly.

It would almost appear as if people were under some obligation to talk whether they had anything to say or not. I refer to this as the chatter of the masses.

If you are not mentally on guard, without noticing it happen, you will be swept into this waste of time and energy.

If you don't consciously and deliberately create order in your mind, your environment, or the people surrounding you, will dictate your mental state.

Observe those who surround you on any given occasion. Their conversation and actions may easily change four or five times in less than a minute.

If you think I am exaggerating, check this out for yourself, or possibly get involved with a few people in conversation and deliberately change the topic as often as possible, over four or five times a minute. If you don't tell them what you are doing, they will never notice but will willingly follow.

What does this mean? Well, your mind is the greatest power in the universe. If you're not diligent, you will waste it and go nowhere. Consciously choose to associate with those great souls who discuss *big* ideas.

A Billionaire's Advice

Last week I quoted Grant Sylvester, the chief operating officer of Money Concepts Canada. He is an author on money matters and a brilliant financial advisor. Yesterday I received an article in the mail from Grant. It is titled "A Billionaire's Simple Secret of Successful Investing." Sounds interesting, doesn't it.? The article is about J. Paul Getty, one of the wealthiest men who ever lived. When he died at age eighty-three, twelve or thirteen years ago, he had amassed one of the world's great art collections. He also had earned a personal fortune worth about $3 billion. What did Getty know about building wealth and investing for spectacular gains that his contemporaries did not? Several years before he died, Mr. Getty shared his secret. In his autobiography, he explained that whenever he made an investment, he tried to apply this simple principle: "If you want to earn money, really big money, do what nobody else is doing. Buy when everyone else is selling and hold until everyone else is buying."

This is not merely a catch slogan. It is the very essence of successful investment. It is probably the simplest, sanest, most powerful and reliable money-making technique ever devised. It works in any market—from gold and silver to stocks, bonds, currencies, real estate, collectibles, or any other market that interests you—because human nature is the same everywhere. You don't need special academic training, but you do require an independent mind and an ounce of courage. Train yourself to buy when everybody, including yourself, is feeling discouraged—when the news is bad. Sell when everybody is excited—when the news is good.

Getty said you need an ounce of courage; it's probably more like a pound you need.

Friendship

Someone once said that friendship consists in forgetting what one has given and remembering what one has received. Too many people waste their time by feeling ignored or slighted because they haven't received a thank you from someone they feel owes them. They would be wise to rise above that childishness.

About seventeen centuries ago the great Roman emperor Marcus Aurelius wrote in *The Meditations*, "Some men, when they do a kindness, ask for the payment of gratitude; others, more modest, remember the favor and look upon you as their debtor. But there are other benefactors who forget their good deeds; and these are like the vine, which is satisfied with being fruitful in its kind, and bears a bunch of grapes without expecting any thanks for it."

The great emperor added to those words saying, "A truly kind man never talks of a good turn he has done, but does another as soon as he can, just like a vine that bears again the next season."

That is pretty sound advice even if it is seventeen centuries old. Dr. David Fink, the neuropsychiatrist said, "We often create needless frustrations for ourselves when we impose selfish and unnecessary, and sometimes, impossible demands and requirements upon others. When those demands and requirements are not met in the way and at the time we want them to be, we become frustrated. And we did it."

This whole idea of giving with no thought of getting in return was the basis of Lloyd C. Douglas's book *Magnificent Obsession*. It may be a tough thing to do, but it is worth working at. You will be a real friend, not to mention the many other forms of compensation you will receive for your new lawful habit.

Will You Pay the Price?

True success is definitely not easy to come by, although it should be. If we all received the proper programming as infants, success would be natural. But it is not. In fact, success is anything but natural. If success is something you are seeking, you must be prepared to pay the price.

The following ten questions came up in an article titled, "Who'll Pay the Price." Test yourself. If you have a sincere desire to become a success in your chosen endeavor, you must be able to answer yes to the following ten questions.

1. You want success—are you willing to pay the price?

2. Can you take a beating and keep pursuing your goal?

3. Is discouragement something you can stand?

4. Can you hang on in the face of obstacles?

5. Are you strong on the finish as well as quick at the start?

6. Have you the grit to do what others have failed to do?

7. Have you the persistence to keep on trying after repeated failures?

8. Have you the nerve to attempt things the average person would never dream of doing?

9. Can you go up against skepticism, ridicule, and friendly advice to quit without flinching?

10. Can you keep your mind steadily on the single objective you are pursuing—resisting all temptations to divide your attention?

Success is sold in the open market. Anyone can buy it who is willing to pay the price. Those questions should be given to every person who is planning to open a new business or accept a position in commissioned sales. The rewards for success are great and are enjoyed by the person who is prepared to pay the price.

It Takes Time

Before he became one of the best-loved presidents of the United States of America, James Garfield was the principal of Hiram College in Ohio—a college designed to give youngsters from the farms of the Western Reserve the chance of an academic education.

One father brought along his son and wanted to see the syllabus—the usual preparatory course lasted four years. After inspecting it, he said, "Mr. Garfield, I don't believe my son will have time to take all that. Could you provide him with a shorter course?"

"Yes, I think I can," replied Garfield. "You see, it all depends on what you want to make of him. When God wants to make an oak, He takes hundreds of years; but when He wants to make a vegetable plant, it requires only three months."

President Garfield gave the father of the young student an interesting answer to a question that occupies the minds of many people. How can I get an education in a shorter period of time?

The answer Garfield gave applies regardless of who is asking the question. It depends on what you want to make of yourself. To master anything takes a long time. You must be forever learning. Education is a lifelong pursuit; it never ends. Those among us who do not understand this basic truth about life, remain stuck, generally in a reasonably dull, uninteresting, and unrewarding position.

The real giants in any profession understand that much like the oak, if they are going to become strong and productive, it will take time. However, in the final analysis, it will be time well spent. Learning can and will be an interesting adventure when you approach it with a positive attitude and your goal in mind.

Become More Creative

There is something good about everything. Anyone who understands the law of opposites or the law of polarity knows this rule to be true. The good side of bad times is that you are forced to become more creative.

I was in a meeting with Keith Watters last week. Keith is in the mortgage business. There are more than a few mortgage brokers in the marketplace who will tell you times are tough right now. Apparently Keith Watters doesn't see it that way. He thinks business is pretty good, but as he puts it, "You sure have to be creative."

It's people like Keith who keep the economy moving until it gets back on the right track. If everyone sat back and cried about bad times, the economy would come to a slow, screeching halt. When Keith left our office, my assistant Gina Robichaud said, "That man always has a good attitude," and he does.

You must have a winning attitude to win, whether the economy is good or bad. The beautiful part of all this is that attitude and creativity are something each of us can control. If you form an image in your mind of how you want your life to be and where you want to go, you can then begin to mentally search for ways of creating the good that you desire.

It isn't necessary to sit and wait for something outside of you to improve. You have been gifted with the mental faculties within you to improve any circumstance around you. However, you must choose to do so.

Do as Keith Watters is doing—become more creative. Check your attitude, as it will ultimately determine your altitude.

163

The Opposite of Courage Is Conformity

If you want to succeed, you must be different from the masses. Be yourself. Do not be afraid to assert your true personality. Don't ever forget that you are a unique individual. As soon as you tow the line, you are denying your true personality and virtually denying yourself the opportunity to grow.

Although society in general has done an excellent job of turning most of us into clones by eliminating difference and nipping our personal aspirations in the bud, a tiny inner voice nevertheless survives within each of us. Timid and worried, it whispers to us that our public images are false, that our genuine personalities are hidden and unexpressed. Frustration, sadness, and in some cases, a feeling of being dead inside, are some of the disadvantages we heap upon ourselves.

The fear of being different and the need to conform are false and destructive. It is an acquired concept, not something we were born with. Here are five powerful affirmations. Read these affirmations aloud a number of times every day for thirty days.

- **Day after day I am asserting my true personality more and more.**

- **I am unique and feel completely free to express my desire to succeed.**

- **It is my right and duty to be myself.**

- The success I achieve will be in keeping with the extent to which I assert myself.

- I am asserting myself more and more in all areas of my life.

- Every day I am increasing my self-worth ten fold and becoming more and more successful.

Repeating these affirmations on a daily basis will develop courage. The opposite of courage is not cowardice; the opposite of courage is conformity. Be yourself. Dare to win.

Note from Author:

I would recommend reading this lesson often. It would be a common but false assumption to think that, since I was raised by Bob Proctor, I would naturally be a product of his teaching. I fell into the trap of conformity all the while knowing my dad's material. Going against the grain and thinking *continued deliberate positive* thought is truly the most laborious thing you will do. Physical labour is much easier.

Be a Winner

This show frequently deals with winning or winners. I recently received a fax from Chris Dimson, a manager at Mister Transmission. Chris shared an article with me entitled "Be a Winner." I would like to share it with you.

> The Winner: Always has a part of the answer.
> The Loser: Always has a part of the problem.
>
> The Winner: Always has a program.
> The Loser: Always has an excuse.
>
> The Winner: Says, "Let me do that for you."
> The Loser: Says, "That's not my job."
>
> The Winner: Sees an answer for every problem.
> The Loser: Sees a problem in every answer.
>
> The Winner: Sees a green near every sand trap.
> The Loser: Sees 3 or 4 sand traps near every green.
>
> The Winner: Says, "It may be difficult to do but it's possible."
> The Loser: Says, "It may be possible, but it's too difficult."

Thanks Chris from all of us who will benefit from your sharing.

I wasn't surprised to receive this article from Chris Dimson, as sharing and caring is part of the philosophy that Chris's company has been built upon. Mister Transmission, as a company, is a great Canadian success story. The company had a very modest beginning, and today they do millions of dollars in business every year. Its owners and executives care about their people. They encourage goal setting and personal development.

Their president has hired my company on several occasions to work with their people. They are well aware that if they help their people get what they want, their people will give them everything the company wants.

If your company is experiencing difficult times, you might think of this: Being a winner is never an accident. Winning comes about by design, determination, and positive action.

Temporary Defeat

Under ordinary circumstances the word "failure" has a very negative connotation. Today I would like to give this word new meaning because it has been frequently misused in the past. The word failure has brought an untold amount of grief and hardship to millions of people.

First and foremost, it is important to distinguish between failure and temporary defeat. Sir Edmund Hillary failed in the eyes of many people in 1951 and again in 1952, in his attempt to climb Mount Everest. However, in Ed Hillary's mind, he had merely met with temporary defeat. No doubt they were disappointing and costly setbacks, but not failures because in 1953, he and Tenzing Norgay, his Sherpa guide, were the first people to reach the 29,028-foot summit of Mount Everest.

Temporary defeats are often a blessing in disguise. They have a tendency to bring us up with a jerk and to cause us to redirect our energies along different and more desirable paths.

I have a theory that temporary defeat is nature's way of strengthening us and giving us the courage necessary to reach our goals. It takes a lot of courage to view temporary defeat as a blessing in disguise. No one ever got up from the knockout blow of defeat without being stronger and wiser from the experience. You can only be classified as a failure when you refuse to get up and go at it again.

Advancement of all kinds is generally preceded by a crisis; the greater the crisis, the greater the opportunity for advancement.

Eliminate the word failure from your vocabulary. You can always get up and go at it again tomorrow. There is no problem outside of you that is superior to the power within you.

Good Times Are Here

Are you aware of all the bad news flying around lately? Politicians, economists, and business leaders are preaching bad times are coming, things are going to get worse. If you are not careful, you will become mentally infected with this doom and gloom. Negative energy like that is more contagious than smallpox.

Make an irrevocable decision this very moment that you will neither talk about nor listen to any conversation about a bad economy.

Change the economy. There is a beautiful hymn that suggests "Let there be peace and let it begin with me." Paraphrase that line to, "Let there be productivity and let it begin with me." Don't wait for others to change things. Follow James J. Metcalfe's advice in his poem "It's Up to Me."

It's Up to Me

*I get discouraged now and then
When there are clouds of gray,
Until I think about the things
That happened yesterday.*

*I do not mean the day before
Or those of months ago,
But all the yesterdays in which
I had the chance to grow.*

I think of opportunities
That I allowed to die,
And those I took advantage of
Before they passed me by.

And I remember that the past
Presented quite a plight,
But somehow I endured it and
The future seemed all right.

And I remind myself that I
Am capable and free,
And my success and happiness
Are really up to me.

The economy or your business will be whatever you decide it will be. If the going is tough, the reward will be great. Contrary to popular belief, you and I are in charge of our results. I have decided this year is going to be tremendous. Why don't you do the same?

You Can—Today

Everyday you and I are being bombarded with negatives. Politics, prices, the economy, interest rates—you name it, we're hearing about it … bad news. Supreme mental strength is required to keep your mind on a track that will lead to a positive end result.

Now is an excellent time to bury your nose in a few history books. You will find the stories of men and women who have continued to win, in spite of what was happening all around them. There have always been personalities who took the economic environment as it existed in their day, and instead of letting it walk on them, as most of us do, they grabbed it by the neck and beat it into submission. Successful business people have always done that and always will. Regardless of what the economic environment was like, some people have figured out how to beat it. There is, as it turns out, always a way. This optimistic statement seems worth expanding on.

In every era, including our own, people have tended to believe that the day of great wealth-gathering opportunities are over. The era that just passed always looked better. Today people complain that high taxes, high prices, high labor costs, and numerous other problems prevent them from making it.

When the first nomadic tribes settled down to cultivate farms at the dawn of human history, there were wandering hunters who went around grumbling that the world was all staked out—forget it. It is equally probable that people in the twenty-first century will gloomily contemplate whatever economic problems beset them, saying, "You can't make it today. If only we were back in the 1970s."

Do as winners have always done and accentuate the positive. Get on the "I can" mental frequency!

Double Your Business

Thomas Carlyle explained that once your mind has been expanded by a big idea, it will never go back to its original state. I like that thought.

For some strange reason, most individuals mentally fool around with a small idea when they begin to think of increasing their business. If they even consider an increase, it is 5, 10, or maybe 15 percent. I want to suggest that you begin to think of doubling your business. That's right. Doubling it.

If you are the chairman of Exxon or some other multinational corporation, the idea is probably ridiculous. However, odds are, you are not in that position. Even if you are, you can double your effectiveness.

Think with me for a moment. It takes no more energy to work on a big idea than it does to work on a small one, so you can proceed assured that this type of mental activity will not give you a brain hemorrhage.

Take a sheet of paper and put a figure at the top that will represent twice the business you are presently doing. If you are in a position where your effectiveness is not measured in dollars, write down what you would be doing if you were twice as effective. Then write the words "How can I?" When you begin to think about this, ideas will probably begin flying into your mind explaining why you can't. They will, in all probability, be valid, but counterproductive. Forget them. Tell yourself you have nowhere to write them. Keep thinking. After a while positive ideas will begin to flow. Write all of them on your paper, even the ridiculous ones.

These positive ideas will prime your pump for better ideas. Al Spizzirri, a friend of mine in Toronto took his income from $18,000 a year to $500,000 in two short years with this concept.

Our seminar company expanded across Canada into all of the USA, Australia, and New Zealand by using it.

Double your business—it's an exciting idea.

Meet the Giants

Everyone admires someone for one reason or another. Quite often the individuals we admire are people we read about but never meet.

The other evening I was having dinner with a friend. We were barbecuing in our backyard, and Andrew Young's name came up. Young was one of the inside workers with Martin Luther King Jr., who later went on to become the American ambassador to the United Nations and then the mayor of Atlanta, Georgia. I have followed his work and his career for years. I see him as a very wise, sincere, service-oriented individual. A person I would certainly enjoy meeting.

My friend mentioned he knew Andrew Young; he had worked with him on a few occasions. I immediately got a commitment from my friend to arrange a meeting with Young; I will definitely go out of my way to meet him.

Too often we admire a person for one reason or another but think it out of our reach to meet them. We may see these people who are in positions of power or authority as being inaccessible, and that is not so.

The next time you catch yourself saying you would really like to meet him or her, do it. Don't think you can't; just think of how you can, and do it.

In the early sixties I flew to Chicago and spent an hour with Earl Nightingale. That meeting ultimately led me to completely change the course of my life. I eventually moved to Chicago and worked with Earl Nightingale for a number of years.

We had the pleasure of having Hugh O'Brian of Wyatt Earp as a guest in our home a couple of years ago. He explained how he went to Africa to meet Albert Schweitzer. That meeting resulted in O'Brian starting the Hugh O'Brian Youth Organization, which is worldwide today and has helped thousands of young people develop leadership skills.

They are never too big to meet. They are usually beautiful people, and they could change your life. If you admire them, get to know them.

Are You Keeping Up?

It was late in the evening when my wife dropped me off at the airport in Toronto. During the night as she lay sleeping, I was ordering breakfast in London, England. As Linda was getting up and getting ready for work, I was directly over Bucharest, and as she was walking into our office in Toronto, I was looking down on Istanbul and the Black Sea. Before she leaves at the end of her business day, I will have been to Bombay and Singapore. I will arrive at my hotel in Kuala Lumpur just about the time she is sitting down to dinner.

Those are the thoughts that are crossing my mind as I make my way around the world. The universe is tightening up. We are living in a rapidly changing world, and the rate of change is exhilarating. The imaginations of world leaders are being challenged today. The individuals who are not willing and prepared to move into high gear with their thinking today are going to be in serious difficulty tomorrow. Those who voice the opinion that the changes taking place in the world mean nothing to them are advertising their ignorance. Everyone is being affected.

You and I must begin to exercise our mental machinery. Change and innovation are the hallmarks of our time. The way we did business last year is not good enough this year. We must think of how to do it better and faster; if we don't, someone else will.

You and I possess the potential to adapt to change and even enjoy it. These are exciting times. Make up your mind right now to involve yourself in a planned program of personal development and prepare yourself to adapt, grow, and enjoy an exciting future.

Take Responsibility

The winners in life can make strong decisions and live by them. They don't shun responsibility. President Jimmy Carter is one such individual. On April 25, 1980, fifty American hostages had been in captivity for 173 days. The president of the United States appeared on television to disclose the failed military attempt to rescue the hostages. After President Carter described the events that led to the aborted mission, he stated, "It was my decision to attempt the rescue operation. It was my decision to cancel it when problems developed. The responsibility is fully my own."

Decision-making undoubtedly is one of the most critical of all leadership functions. It requires tremendous internal courage. Lack of courage in this area has been the downfall of many otherwise very successful people. There is nothing more frustrating than having to deal with a weak-minded person who refuses to be decisive.

At times, we are all tempted to make rather ridiculous excuses to others. If we would consciously examine our excuses, we would discover how ridiculous most of them sound. Listen to a few choice excuses that were offered in relation to automobile accidents:

An invisible car came out of nowhere, struck my car, and vanished.

I had been driving my car for forty years when I fell asleep at the wheel and had the accident.

I pulled away from the side of the road, lunged at my mother-in-law, and headed over the embankment.

If you are faced with some big decisions, take the bull by the horn. Understand that you have tremendous abilities. You can develop courage and strength to take responsibility for your actions.

This chapter comes from Gerry Robert's book, *Conquering Life's Obstacles*. I'd suggest that you add it to your library!

Frequencies of Thought

"The significant problems we face cannot be solved at the same level of thinking we were at when we created them."

Permit me to repeat that because it is a mighty important observation made by Albert Einstein. "The significant problems we face cannot be solved at the same level of thinking we were at when we created them."

The way you see the problem is the problem. Some time ago I was conducting a management seminar. The audience was comprised of seventy-five senior supervisors. A gentleman in the audience asked this question: "What do you do with an obnoxious person?" This manager's thinking led him to believe the individual he was managing was obnoxious. Before the manager could solve the problem, he had to adjust his own thinking. I suggested that the person in question was beautiful.

There is something quite amazing about every person including this one; it was his behavior that was obnoxious. The manager should have been asking himself what was causing the person to behave in such an obnoxious manner. A person's behavior is an expression of his or her self-image, so this is where the manager needed to start.

The truth is not always in the appearance of things. Whatever we see on the outside is a symptom or an effect. The cause is on the inside. The answers to all of our problems are inside not outside. As we study and observe our own behavior, we will begin to see this truth. Then we will quickly recognize it is the same with others. Thinking from the inside out rather than from the outside in will put you in charge of your life. Then other people and circumstances will cease to be the source of your problems.

183

You Need to Know

I have a beauty for you today. This reading is an upper if you happen to be on a downer.

The message is clear: don't permit anything to keep you down. Walter Brenan shared the following with us:

> A person needs to know that they're bad and they're good.
> You can be what you hope, you can be understood.
> A person needs to feel they can conquer a fall,
> For a person who can kneel has the strength to stand tall.
>
> A person needs to know they can share and confide,
> Even though they're frightened way down deep inside.
> For sometimes a person will sink terribly low,
> Before they discover how high they can go.
>
> A person needs to know at the end of their rope,
> They can handle their fears, they can build on their hope.
> A person must believe they can change when they must.
> They can learn to receive, they can learn to trust.
>
> And why should a person feel afraid and alone,
> When each of us has the same fears of his own.
> For sometimes a person must sink terribly low,
> Before they discover how high they can go.
>
> A person has to live when it's painful to try,
> For a person needs to laugh and a person needs to cry.
> A person has a need to strive and prevail.
> They must learn to succeed and find out why they fail.

To carry your crown and to fill up your cup,
Sometimes you will drop down, so you can reach up.
For sometimes a person must sink terribly low,
Before he discovers how high he can go.

If you have friends who are down, send them a copy of this.
They will thank you.

Natural Goal Achiever

Do you ever think of yourself as a natural goal achiever? If you don't, you should because you are … a natural goal achiever.

The moment the first breath of life filled your lungs, you set out pursuing goals. You are innately programmed to improve the quality of your life. Each of your early achievements brought with them tremendous satisfaction, along with great pride and joy.

Your first goal was to get something to eat, and where have you ever seen anyone more satisfied than a baby who has just been fed? Where have you seen greater pride and joy than on the face of a new mother nursing her baby?

How about those other early goals—to crawl, to talk, or walk. Think of the satisfaction, pride, and joy that came with the first word or first step. The satisfaction of the first word or step soon wears off, and dissatisfaction sets in. You want to put words together, steps together. They became goals, and, as you accomplished them, more satisfaction, pride, and joy followed, but so did the feeling of dissatisfaction. You wanted to accomplish more, do greater things.

You naturally want to experience life and experience it in abundance. You not only should, you *can* have the things you want—all of them—and you will have them if you rekindle that early spirit that caused you to pursue and achieve those first goals.

Unfortunately, too many of us were told at an early stage that we should be satisfied with what we had. Goals and their importance were lost.

You should never be satisfied—happy, but not satisfied. Dissatisfaction is a creative state. It took you out of the cave and put you into the condominium. It gave you the wheel, the fax, and the furnace. Dissatisfaction gave you and me a lifestyle that is the envy of the world.

Develop a healthy dissatisfaction with your life. Set new goals—big, exciting goals. Then, set out to achieve them with the same enthusiasm you knew and used as a baby. That is called living; everything else is dying.

Be Merciful and Work

Gina Robichaud attempts to keep me organized and helps me get to where I'm going, whether it's Albany, New Zealand, or Albany, New York. Gina recently gave me a real jewel. It is a beautiful leather-bound book written 120 years ago by John Ruskin.

Here are a few lines from Ruskin's writings.

He wrote that "however good you may be, you have faults; that however dull you may be, you can find out what some of them are; and that however slight they may be, you had better make some—not too painful, but patient—effort to get rid of them. Trust me for this, that whatever you may find or fancy your faults to be, there are only two that are of real consequence,—Idleness and Cruelty. Perhaps you may be proud. Well, we can get much good out of pride, if only it not be not religious. Perhaps you may be vain: it is highly probable; and very pleasant for the people who like to praise you. Perhaps you are a little envious: that is really very shocking; but then—so is everybody else. Perhaps, also, you are a little malicious, which I am truly concerned to hear, but should probably, if I knew you, enjoy your conversation. But whatever else you may be, you must not be useless, and you must not be cruel. If there is any one point which, in six thousand years of thinking about right and wrong, wise and good people have agreed upon, and by experience discovered, it is that God dislikes idle and cruel people more

189

than any other—that His first order is, 'Work while you have light.' His second is, 'Be merciful while you have mercy.'

It may be 120 years old, but it is good advice.

Note from Author:

Gina does keep dad organized and has been doing so since I was in high school. She does an incredible job and is really a part of our family.

The Boys Down at the Stable

If you want to win, stay away from the losers! Here is a story that is priceless.

"Once upon a time there was a fellow by the name of Al Capp who wrote a comic strip called L'il Abner. Many years ago he had some characters in his strip who lived in a town near Dogpatch. They were the town bums, the ne'er do wells, the failures whose whole aim in life was to pass judgment on others. Their criticism and ridicule became so vehement that, in time, the rest of the people in the town became acutely conscious of it. The boys down at the stable, as they were called because that's where they spent most of their time, soon set the social standards of the town. Nobody could do anything without their sanction.

"Because they lived within the structure of their crummy little world, they would laugh and point their fingers at anyone and everyone who tried to be better than they were. As a result, the people feared the ridicule of the boys down at the stable so much that they stopped trying. Soon everybody became bums and the town died.

"In every social structure, whether it be family, town, county, or state, there are the boys down at the stable. They are the jealous ones. They are too scared to try something different. They show their ignorance by laughing at those who do. Learn to recognize them for what they are. Don't let them hurt you. It takes a certain amount of toughness to succeed. One has to rise above those who would tear you down so that they can laugh and say, 'I told you so!'"

Licked? Tired? Broke?

Have you had a bad week? Perhaps you're a little tired, or maybe you're broke.

When you don't get the breaks and the defeats pile up, when you're discouraged and don't care about the future, when you're ready to toss in the sponge and quit, take a minute to consider this man's record:

Failed in business	....	1831
Defeated for legislature	....	1832
Failed in business again	....	1833
Elected to legislature	....	1834
Sweetheart died	....	1835
Nervous breakdown	....	1836
Defeated for speaker	....	1838
Defeated for land officer	....	1843
Defeated for congress	....	1843
Elected to congress	....	1846
Defeated for re-election	....	1848
Defeated for senate	....	1855
Defeated for vice president	....	1856
Defeated for senate	....	1858
Elected president	....	1860

Who was he? An obscure country boy without any education, who refused to let it handicap him. He refused to remain obscure. He refused to stay uneducated—he educated himself. He refused to plead hard luck. He refused to accept failure. He refused to turn back when all the odds seemed hopeless. He believed in, and practiced, simplicity, honesty, industry, persistence, tolerance, friendliness and faith.

He was Abraham Lincoln.

He won and so can you! Keep going

Thought Plus Action

Successful living consists of knowing and being. When the two are separated, there is nothing but frustration and failure. To know all about love without loving can be disastrous. Knowing all about the right way to live and not acting on what you know, on a daily basis, can prove to be very destructive for everyone.

Unfortunately, most of the self-help books on our bestseller lists deal with positive thinking without much concern for translating it consciously into experience. We are supplied with maps to Nirvana but cannot locate the vehicle to get us there.

If positive thinking alone resulted in successful living, 95 percent of our population would reside on easy street. All of our preachers and teachers would be physical examples of health, wealth, and well-being. Unfortunately, many are physical contradictions to what they tell us.

Half-truths are more elusive than lies. Positive thinking as a medium to the good life is just that, a half-truth.

Positive thinking alone does not deliver, it does not fulfill; in fact, it frustrates because it is not in harmony with what we do. Thinking positively about music will not make you a musician. Only singing and playing a musical instrument will bring you fulfillment.

The power of positive thought lies in its being expressed in a positive act. The thought of love finds its fulfillment in loving. Thoughts of joy find their power in laughter. Faith without action is dead. Nothing can have such negative results as positive thinking without the action that fulfills that thinking.

Schools should award diplomas for what we do rather than what we know. Nothing is more powerful than a positive thought joined with positive action.

Note from Author:

This lesson is profound. Most of the naysayers of *The Secret* do not understand this part of the equation. Wishing does not attract what you want. Continuously thinking about what you want and believing in it will position you to act toward your desire. If you do not act, however, your wants will not appear.

Daily Little Tasks

If you happen to be like most people, there are very likely a number of activities you are involved with every day that are becoming monotonous. These of course are habitual, routine activities that you are called upon to do each day, some of which you may not even enjoy performing. Well, don't despair because there is a way you can add a shot of enthusiasm to these activities, which will, in turn, add pleasure to your work.

Arthur Rubenstein, the famous pianist, lived to be ninety-five years old and was still performing in public when he was ninety. Anyone who watched him playing could easily see that Mr. Rubenstein got enormous joy out of his work.

One day he was asked about the secret of his exuberance: how could he play pieces so enthusiastically that he must have played so many hundreds of times before? Rubenstein replied, "I try to imagine I am playing each piece for the very first time, so the music comes new to me every time."

That is a principle you and I could apply to many aspects of our lives. Think of the boredom that would be eliminated with that type of attitude.

Yule Brenner played the role of the King of Siam thousands of times on stage, repeating the same lines over and over, night after night. Every time he stepped onto the stage, he fascinated and inspired his audience with a magnificent performance.

In his writings, Wallace D. Wattles said, "You become great by doing little things in a great way every day."

I know for a fact that if you make that principle a habit, as many true professionals have done, you will be milestones ahead of the masses. Start today!

Everybody Has a Book in Them

Have you ever thought of writing a book? The thought has probably crossed your mind. For years I honestly believed that writers were different. It was as if they had been touched by some capricious God and endowed with special talent the rest of us would never enjoy.

But in the late seventies I was working out of Los Angeles, and the subject of writing a book popped up during a general conversation in our office. John DeMarco, one of my associates said, "Everyone has a book in them."

For some reason that suggestion stuck in my mind. Everyone has a book in them. Every now and then those words would play in my mind like a broken record. A couple of years later I published a book, which, to my good fortune, has become a bestseller in Canada. Naturally, DeMarco's suggestion has my support today, and I have repeated it to others before you.

Some time ago I was having lunch with a very successful Toronto businessman. The subject of books came up and I said, "Everybody has a book in them." Well, since then he has written two books; the first one was a selling sensation in Canada in 1985 and sold over a million copies in hardcover in Japan. It has been translated into eight different languages.

G. Kingsley Ward's latest book, *Letters of a Businessman to His Daughter*, was released in the past few months, and it looks like another smash hit. Kingsley Ward probably never thought of himself as an author.

How about you? If you want to have some fun and learn something about yourself, you might try to prove that John DeMarco was right.

Note from Author:

Wow, this story brought back a long-forgotten memory. I always dreamed of obtaining my pilot licence. When I was young my dad had me meet with King Ward at his pharmaceutical company to ask him about flying. King Ward had his private pilot licence. He took the time to answer all of my questions and gave me two books: one on flying and an autographed copy of his book. I clearly have not made the decision to fly as I am still without my licence. I think I might just change that. Dad is right (again). Everyone has a book in them. Start to write your book today.

Start Your Own Business

The other day I was talking with a young man who will graduate from university next month. He was having a very difficult time making a decision with respect to his future employment. What would he do? Where would he go? On and on the questions flowed. However, the answers were escaping him.

I began by asking him how he wanted to live and where he wanted to live. Then I asked how much he wanted to earn. The amount he wanted to earn was considerably more than what 99 percent of the companies in the country would offer if they decided to employ him.

Then I asked, "Why don't you start your own company? Work for yourself?" I suggested that every company in the world was started by someone. If they could do it, he could too.

His reply was a blank stare; then slowly he said, "I never thought of that."

I replied, "There are millions of people in the country, and every one of them has needs. Think of what those needs are, then, which one you would most enjoy filling."

For some strange reason, as a people, we seem to think that you must be a certain age before you can start a business of your own. That idea has no foundation—it's ridiculous! Age has nothing to do with starting a business. Courage, ambition, and a sincere desire to serve others is all that is required. You may be eighteen or eighty.

I recently read that Kemins Wilson is building a new chain of hotels—Wilson Inns. Mr. Wilson is eighty years old. He was retired and became bored; by the way, he is the originator of the Holiday Inns.

Young Tim Dorchuk of Burlington, Ontario, at nineteen is a self-made millionaire. He started his own business at the age of twelve.

Experience—you will get it. Money—you will attract it. Make a decision, find a need, and fill it. Your age should not be a consideration.

Choose Your Grades

Noele Wrycraft is a lovely young lady who has been working in our office for the past two summers while school was out. She will soon be returning to Western University, and everyone will miss Noele's pleasant personality breezing around the office.

I asked Noele, "If you could write your own report card for the coming year, what marks would you give yourself?" She paused, smiled, and replied, "A's."

I said, "All A's?"

She replied, "Yes."

I asked why she didn't write her own report card, to which she replied, "I can't do that; the school writes my report card."

In wanting to get a point across to Noele, I asked what her dad worked at. She said he was a sales manager for a data processing company. I then asked Noele to phone her dad and ask him when his fiscal year started, and whether, prior to the start of his year, he had a written plan stating what his sales would be.

Noele called him, and he told her that his fiscal year began in January, and yes, he knew in November what their target was for the coming year.

I suggested to Noele that since her dad wrote his own report card before his year began that she should try doing the same. I know she will; Noele Wrycraft is a sharp young lady.

Write your own report card. At the end of each term or semester, you're able to see what has been done relative to what you want. You will know what adjustments are necessary, if any are required.

Writing your own report card before school begins beats waiting and wondering. Choose your grades, then, just think of how you can (not excuses of why you can't). You'll be a winner!

Problems Are Mental in Nature

In Raymond Holliwell's book *Working with the Law*, the author suggests that our problems are mental in nature. They have no existence outside of themselves, and it has been discovered that nearly all will yield up their solutions when subjected to a broad and exact analysis. Holliwell went on to suggest that you and I should have good sound reasons for all of the views we hold. As we try to find these, many of our old time views will fall to pieces. We should form clear and definite ideas regarding our convictions as to why we do as we do and as to why we think as we think. That is excellent advice.

Another author said essentially the same thing when he said, "It ain't what a person don't know that hurts them, it's what they know that ain't so that hurts them." So true. Most of us buy into false concepts. In last night's edition of the *Toronto Star* a Gallup Poll of 1003 adults was published on what those people believed was the cause of stress in their lives. More than 50 percent of people under 50 years of age believed that money and their jobs were the cause of their problems. Those people should definitely follow Holliwell's advice and examine their beliefs. They could eliminate much of their stress. Jobs and money are never the primary cause of stress. Thinking—negative thinking—causes stress. The real cause of all problems lies in our thoughts, not in things or circumstances. You and I possess the power to change our thoughts. It is our greatest power—the power to choose. If you are feeling stressed, choose to relax. Look at your problems as a stranger might. Then do something about them—*now!*

Worry

Worry is a psychic disease that has become a national pastime. You should also understand it is more contagious than smallpox.

Worry causes you to become very lethargic and irritable, in other words, very poor company. Worry is the forerunner to fear, which causes anxiety and ultimately physical disease.

You will never, let me repeat, never witness any truly productive behavior expressed from a worried mind. You should not mistake worry for a conscious concern; there is a vast difference in the two. You are worrying when you choose negative thoughts and direct them toward a particular end.

Permit me to give you an excellent example. A number of years ago I was living and working in Los Angeles. I had occasion to be in Toronto, and I was visiting a friend. He was in a very poor frame of mind, not at all a pleasant person to be around. That wasn't too bad for me; I was just visiting. His family was in a much different position.

I asked his wife what the problem was, and she explained he was worried sick because he was $2,000 short to meet his payroll the following week. I spoke to him and said a lot could happen in a week, don't worry. That didn't help. I took a checkbook from a Canadian bank and gave him a check for $2,000. I said, "If you don't use it, Don, give the check back to me when I return." His personality changed instantly. He was happy.

The following month Don returned the same check saying he did not have to use it. I replied, "That's good, Don, because there was no money in that account."

Ninety-three percent of what you worry about never happens. Don't worry, be happy! Be happy!

Eliminate Excuses

A number of years ago I conducted a series of personal development seminars for a large insurance company in the United States. A couple of months after the seminars were completed, I was invited by John Lasater to speak at a special function for his office in downtown Chicago. John's office had been part of the group that attended the seminars, and they were enjoying tremendous success with their sales. I asked John what he considered to be the greatest benefit of the seminars. I was almost certain that he would say the additional sales, but he didn't. John replied that the seminars had eliminated excuses. I never forgot that.

Think of how much happier you would be, not to mention how much more productive you would be, if you eliminated excuses. I once read the worst thing that can happen to you is to have an excuse. And, if there is anything worse, it would be to have a good excuse.

When you use an excuse for not accomplishing something or not completing a project, you are actually giving power to someone or something outside of yourself. Because there are some circumstances you cannot change, and you most certainly cannot change other people, you are stuck. There is a power within you that is far superior to any condition or circumstance outside of you.

Here is a great suggestion for you to try. Try it today. Regardless of what happens today, absolutely refuse to use an excuse to get off the hook. That may be difficult; it might even sound silly, but try it anyway.

When excuses are eliminated, productivity goes up and people are happier. Remember ... the very worst thing that can happen to you is to have a good excuse.

To Any Child's Parents

I once heard a great educator say that it would take the average Grade one school teacher about twenty-five years to undo much of the damage that has been done prior to a child entering school. Every thought, word, and action surrounding an infant contributes to the child's subconscious programming. This programming, or conditioning, ultimately determines the direction that the child's life will take. Most of our personal development programs today teach us how to change this old conditioning thereby improving our lives.

Here is a magnificent poem that we have used in our seminars for years, entitled "To Any Child's Parent" that brings the importance of the subject to mind.

There are little eyes upon you
And they're watching night and day;
There are little ears that quickly
Take in everything you say.

There are little hands all eager
To do everything you do;
And a little child who's dreaming
Of the day they'll be like you.

You're the little person's idol;
You're the wisest of the wise.
In their little mind, about you
No suspicions ever rise.

They believe in you devoutly,
Hold all that you say and do,

They will say and do in your way,
When they're grown up, just like you.

There's a wide-eyed little person
Who believes you're always right;
And their ears are always open
And they're watching day and night.

You are setting an example
Every day in all you do;
For the little person who's waiting
To grow up and be like you.

None of us are perfect. There are many areas in our lives that we can improve upon. We should keep in mind that as we improve our thoughts and actions, we are also passing on something of value to our children.

About the Author
Ray Proctor

Ray with Toni and their three sons, Curtis, Ben and Brian.

Ray Proctor was born five short years after his father, Bob Proctor, had been given the book *Think and Grow Rich* by Napoleon Hill. This book had such a profound impact on Bob's life that he named Ray after the gentleman who gave him the book, Raymond Douglas Stanford. Ray carries a deep appreciation for sharing the name of an individual who had such a significant contribution to his father's success.

It may be natural to expect that being raised by the Bestselling Author of *You Were Born Rich*, and star of the hit DVD *The Secret*, that success came naturally to Ray. The truth is that it

213

only comes natural to those who apply the laws of success in a persistent and responsible way no matter who your father may be. Ray was in and out of three different high schools with poor grades before he took some responsibility for his life. He had discovered a university that he wished to attend because he knew it would help him achieve his new life goals; first, he had to return to high school to improve his grades and obtain his diploma. Ray's new focus and clear objectives enabled him to complete this task with ease for the first time in his life. A few years later, Ray graduated from Wilfrid Laurier University with an Economics Degree. He thought he was set as he started out in the real world. After all, he was Bob's son. He soon learned with painful clarity, however, that each of us has to apply the lessons of the laws of success with persistence and responsibility. He also learned that merely wishing for something, like having his own successful business, doesn't make it happen. In a few short years he lost almost everything. The fears he learned from that experience kept him in the corporate world for years to come. Ray excelled in the insurance industry, directing claims operations and teams of litigation specialists but he retreated from taking any other risks.

He was never quite satisfied, however, and he knew he was capable of much greater things.

Ray finally began focusing on his father as someone other than a parent. He studied his father's teachings and made learning a key aspect of his everyday life. The changes in his life were almost immediate. The persistent and responsible application of the laws of success became a staple in his life. No longer was success just a wish. It was a constant intentional thought followed by action. Within six months Ray had more than doubled his income and left the insurance industry behind him. One of his father's partners then approached Ray and asked him if he would be interested in running one of Bob's companies. Ray is now part of the family business as CEO of LifeSuccess Publishing. It is through his experience and appreciation of how much of a difference daily study can make that Ray decided to develop *100 Lessons from My Father.*

Today Ray shares his life with his wife Toni and their three sons, Curtis, Ben and Brian.

For more information on Bob Proctor's teachings, programs, and materials, visit

www.bobproctor.com.